ESCAPING THE

vampire

DESPERATE FOR THE IMMORTAL HERO

KIMBERLY POWERS

David C Cook®
transforming lives together

ESCAPING THE VAMPIRE
Published by David C. Cook
4050 Lee Vance View
Colorado Springs, CO 80918 U.S.A.

David C. Cook Distribution Canada
55 Woodslee Avenue, Paris, Ontario, Canada N3L 3E5

David C. Cook U.K., Kingsway Communications
Eastbourne, East Sussex BN23 6NT, England

David C. Cook and the graphic circle C logo
are registered trademarks of Cook Communications Ministries.

The Web site addresses recommended throughout this book are offered as a
resource to you. These Web sites are not intended in any way to be or imply an
endorsement on the part of David C. Cook, nor do we vouch for their content.

This book is a commentary on the themes found in the *The Twilight
Saga*. This book has not been approved, licensed, endorsed, or sponsored
by Stephenie Meyer or Little, Brown Young Readers.

The names mentioned throughout this book have been changed for privacy purposes.

LCCN 2009935964
ISBN 978-1-4347-0061-2
eISBN 978-1-4347-0072-8

© 2009 Kimberly Powers
Published in association with the literary agency of
D.C. Jacobson & Associates LLC, an Author Management Company
www.dcjacobson.com

The Team: Don Pape, Melanie Larson, Amy Kiechlin,
Sarah Schultz, Caitlyn York, Karen Athen
Cover design: Jason Gabbert, The DesignWorks Group
Cover photo: Steve Gardner, PixelWorks Studios

Printed in the United States of America
First Edition 2009

1 2 3 4 5 6 7 8 9 10

091409

*To my heavenly Father, for Your gracious hand
on my life. Thank You for the gift of sharing Your
amazing, undying love with Your daughters.*

❧

*To my handsome Tim—for your devotion, your
amazingly persistent love, and your support for expressing
my heart for God's glory. Your commitment to our
family continues to inspire me! Thanks for boys' nights
with our two guys and for doing what it takes … you've
carried me through this journey! I love you … FNAE!*

❧

*To my Landon—your heart is so full of love and life.
What an amazing blessing you are in our family.
Your smiles and love delight our hearts! God has
used your words many times throughout the writing
of this book. Conversations and time with you are
priceless gifts … I am so proud of you, and I love
being your mom! Thank you for sharing your mommy
with many teen girls over the years of your life!*

To my Logan—what a sweet gift your life has been to us! You are our precious Logan with a brave and joy-filled heart. Your hugs and "squinting-eye smiles" light up our lives! Your heart and life bring encouragement and hope, and we know your future is filled with greatness. We needed you in our family … I am so proud to be your mommy. Can't wait to share all the adventures of life with you!

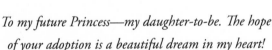

To my future Princess—my daughter-to-be. The hope of your adoption is a beautiful dream in my heart! Our family is waiting with so much love for you!

Let me hear of your unfailing love each
morning, for I am trusting you.
Show me where to walk, for I give myself to you.
Rescue me from my enemies, LORD;
I run to you to hide me. Teach me to do your will,
for you are my God. May your
gracious Spirit lead me forward
on a firm footing.
For the glory of your name, O
LORD, preserve my life.
Because of your faithfulness, bring
me out of this distress.
In your unfailing love, silence all my enemies
and destroy all my foes,
for I am your servant.

(Ps. 143:8–12 NLT)

Contents

Preface

Alone tonight.
Running for her life.
She tears through the woods as fast as she
can, heart beating, trying desperately to
escape the enemy. Questions fill her thoughts.
Where will I find refuge, a place to hide? Is
there anyone out there who can save me?
Fear and panic consume her as the whispering
thoughts dance around her mind. She's
desperate for help, for rescue ... for escape.

∽

If you knew that there was a true hero who could offer you a lasting escape from whatever it is that you're running from—a hero who would walk with you, protect your life, lead you forward, hold you close, and make you strong—wouldn't you want him to desperately search for and rescue you?

"'They will fight against you but will not overcome you, for I am with you and will rescue you,' declares the LORD" (Jer. 1:19 NIV). Christ boldly says that He stands with you and pursues you as your rescuer.

My prayer is that through the pages of this book you will hear the story of the true rescuer. It is this Hero who offers you belonging, mystery, love, excitement, and adventure—all the things we are desperate to find. May you hear His heart for you and be richly encouraged, so empowered by His strength and overwhelmed by His loyalty and love for you!

Throughout the process of writing I have often prayed for you. I have no doubt God has specifically written words for you here—words of rescue, hope, encouragement, love. I'm excited to take this journey with you.

I have been honored to speak to thousands of teen girls at conferences, and I have had the opportunity to share life with them, hear their stories, and pray with them. And even though we can't be together in person right now, throughout the book I've added little moments called "Just Breathe …" where you and I can connect with each other and with God. Sometimes there will be questions to think about; sometimes I might ask you just to take a breath, or smile or take a moment with God. And I do want to hear what the Hero is doing in your life. So please search for *Escaping the Vampire* on Facebook—and send me a message! I believe strongly that God wants to do much inside your life as you read this book. So let these conversations between you and me lead you closer to knowing the heart of your true Immortal Hero—Jesus Christ!

Kimberly

Acknowledgments

What an amazing journey! This book has been a "God thing"—from the very first moment of inspiration, through the many long nights of writing, to everyone who inspired and pushed me along in this journey. I am so thankful to Jesus for the honor of sharing His heart for his daughters through these pages.

My amazing parents—Bob and Pat Sweet—have given their hearts, passed on our Sweet family heritage of faith, and shown me how to love and follow my Lord! My best friend and sister, Tara—your compassion and deep love for God, family, and friends has always inspired me. My brother Rob—your faithful heart and devotion to God and family is a gift. Thanks for your many words throughout this book! My brother Brian—your passion for God, incredible talents, and strong, caring heart point me to the Lord! I thank God for the gifts of Joe, Jodie, and Christie. Our family was not complete without you three!

My dear friend Sheila—your friendship is a precious gift! My wonderful friend Kelly—for your connection with me in heart and prayer at all times! To LaRose, Daisy, Donna, and Kimie for knowing and loving my heart. To family—my loving aunt Gwen, Laura, and Mom II.

Thanks to Melody, Theresa, Christie, Kim S., Leigh, Lori, Francie, Missy, Kathy S., Xandria, Kim and Rick, Carolyn, Dannah, Laura R., Gem, Judy, Whitney, and the many others who have shared our heart and passion for teens! Thanks to Erica for being the first to encourage me to write my heart. Thanks, Ginny, for love and support—and for the writing getaways at Breath of Heaven.

Thanks to my assistant Liz for Starbucks runs, prayers, and your writing talent woven throughout this book!

Many thanks to my literary agency, D. C. Jacobson and Associates. What a tremendous gift you have been—I am so thankful for your professionalism, wisdom, and inspiration. You gave more to this project than I ever could have expected! Thanks for believing in this concept and connecting me with those who can take it to the world. Many thanks to Don Jacobson, Jenni Burke, Lauren, and Penny.

I thank my editor and friend, Steffany Woolsey, for listening to my heart and sharing hours of work, prayer, professionalism, and wisdom throughout these pages! To my editor, Melanie Larson—thank you for sharing your talent and incredible insight, making this book exactly what it needs to be for the girls.

With an incredibly grateful heart I thank the team at David C. Cook—Don Pape for your vision and support, Caitlyn, Ingrid, Douglas, Amy, Sarah, Karen Stoller, and Karen Athen—for all that has gone into making this manuscript a BOOK! Your amazing support is giving wings to this message.

PART I

Illusion Shattered

Let me hear of your unfailing love each morning,
for I am trusting you. Show me where to walk,
for I give myself to you. Rescue me from my
enemies, LORD; I run to you to hide me.

(Ps. 143:8–9 NLT)

CHAPTER 1

Allure of Darkness

Jesus spoke to the people once more and said,
"I am the light of the world. If you follow me,
you won't have to walk in darkness, because
you will have the light that leads to life."

(John 8:12 NLT)

I dug through my purse for my little notebook, squinting in the dim theater light. Attempting to eat popcorn, sip Coke, and frantically write in the dark is not something I suggest. But I *had* to jot down all the thoughts flying through my head about this film that had captured so many hearts.

What could possibly be so appealing about a vampire story? I needed to find out what so many teens were raving about.

As I watched *Twilight*, I waited tensely for a devious, dark villain to appear. But he never showed up—at least, not in the way I expected. Instead I watched Edward, an intriguingly handsome character, sweep the heroine, Bella, off her feet. Edward was Bella's dashing prince, a prince with a bit of modern dark knight. A noble character. Desperate to love and be loved. Charming, and yet ... he was still a vampire.

Does Bella understand that he could kill her at any moment? Or does she even care? In scene after scene, Bella's devotion to Edward deepened. By the movie's end, I found myself intrigued.

As the credits rolled, I gathered my things and dusted popcorn crumbs off my scribbled notes. That's when I noticed dozens of girls still seated, staring at the screen. They wanted more.

IN THE BEGINNING

Several weeks ago, I walked into Borders and saw a long table piled with books on clearance. Near the top was a 960-page, hugely scary-looking paperback titled *The Vampire Book: The Encyclopedia of the Undead.* An evil-looking fanged vampire stared at me from the front cover, begging me not to pick it up.

As I glanced around at shelf after shelf of books, I noticed many titles with the word *vampire* in them. Vampire lit is hot. When and how did this frenzy begin? And what is fueling the excitement over this material?

To be honest, my experience with vampires up to this point was limited. My connection to them before that day was the impression I'd gotten as a five-year-old on Halloween: They were fake, scary, and dangerous. As a result, I've steered clear of the fanged creatures my entire life.

Needless to say, I never dreamed I would pick up a book like

"What is behind this tremendous fascination with vampires? It is likely that there is no simple answer to this question, since the vampire embodies many aspects related to the human condition. These include death (and all of its psychological ramifications), immortality, forbidden sexuality, sexual power and surrender, intimacy, alienation, rebellion, violence, and a fascination with the mysterious."
—*The Vampire Book*[1]

The Vampire Book. But I was in the middle of researching to write this and thought it would be a good resource. So for one entire day I read, highlighted, and learned more about vampires than I ever wished to know.

THE BACKSTORY

What I learned is that vampire mythology has existed for millennia. Ancient cultures including the "Mesopotamians, Hebrews, Ancient Greeks, and Romans had tales of demons and spirits which are considered precursors to modern vampires."[2]

Clearly, this is not a new phenomenon. I think Solomon said it best when he wrote, "There is nothing new under the sun" (Eccl. 1:9 NIV). The same applies to vampires, too.

"Throughout history, vampires have been known ... to be dead humans who returned from the grave and attacked and sucked the blood of the living as a means of sustaining themselves."[3] Wow. That's not a pretty picture! But it certainly matched the image in my head.

I read further. From the sixteenth century onward, the myth of vampires became ingrained into cultural belief systems in eastern Europe. Story after story spread to cultures around the world. Eventually, the idea of vampires "came to the

Literature Grows Fangs

In April 1819, a short story by John Polidori called "The Vampyre" was published in *New Monthly Magazine.* It is considered the foundation of modern vampire fiction.

Toward the end of the nineteenth century, the novel *Dracula* by Bram Stoker ushered in the popular era of vampire fiction that continues to this day. Stoker drew heavily upon the accounts of mythical vampires in Transylvania and Romania.

attention of both the scholarly community and the public in the West because of such creatures in Eastern Europe in the seventeenth and eighteenth centuries."[4]

Vampire films gained popularity in the twentieth and twenty-first century, the most prominent of which was Universal Pictures' *Dracula* (1979). Well-known actors and actresses rose to fame in vampire-themed TV shows and movies: Alex O'Loughlin in *Moonlight,* Sarah Michelle Gellar in *Buffy the Vampire Slayer,* Kiefer Sutherland in *The Lost Boys,* Brad Pitt and Tom Cruise in *Interview with the Vampire.* Most recently, the HBO drama series *True Blood* has captivated millions of viewers (3.7 million watched the second-season premiere).

The end of the twentieth century and beginning of the twenty-first surged with interest in vampire books, movies, TV shows, magazines, and Web sites—the Vampire Academy series, *Buffy the Vampire Slayer,* The Morganville Vampires series, *True Blood,* and *Blade,* to name just a few.

And then came *Twilight.* Since 2005, Stephenie Meyer's breakout series about a family of morally upright vampires living in Forks, Washington, has sold more than 42 million copies with translations into thirty-seven languages around the globe.

These upright vampires are a part of the most recent portrayal of "good-guy vampires" established in fiction literature and media over the last fifty years.

And what exactly is a good-guy vampire? Margaret L. Carter, a scholar of vampire literature, defines them as "vampires who act morally when dealing with mortals, and, as a whole, conform their moral perspective to a human ethical perspective."[5]

Many readers and moviegoers have become even more intrigued by this new image.

Just breathe ...

So what do you think about this "new image" of good vampires? Does it change the way you see them in your head?

At this point, I felt like I had a basic understanding of vampire mythology's roots and its rise in popular culture. The problem was, I still didn't understand why it was such a hot trend today. I had to know more.

I got my answer from an article quoting Ken Gelder, author of *Reading the Vampire:* "'America has taken the vampire story and tied it to teen romance.' Rather than being attracted to the darkness of the vampire, the female leads love their fanged paramours for their essentially decent personalities—along with their bad-boy allure—and are able to get beyond the whole lust-for-blood thing."[6]

> "The continuing popularity of the vampire theme has been ascribed to a combination of two factors: the representation of sexuality and the perennial dread of mortality."—Wikipedia.org[7]

This, finally, made sense to me. After all, good girls attracted to bad boys is an old story. The promise of excitement and the allure of danger is an appealing combination, particularly if there is a chance for redemption.

It also explained how something so obviously evil as a vampire could become the hero of a love story. After all, what could be more impossible—or irresistible—than a devastatingly handsome, reformed vampire? Right there is the formula for a captivating love story. It's Romeo and Juliet (plus fangs) all over again.

A CLOSER LOOK

In 2008, the four *Twilight* books were the top four novels on *USA TODAY*'s best-selling books list. I recently received an email from a conference attendee named Trina, an avid fan of the *Twilight* series. Her analysis of the characters and story was so honest and eye-opening to me that I asked to share her words with you in this book. I think you'll see, as I did, how her examination of the books reveals the longing heart that beats inside each of us for a hero and a protector.

To: Kimberly

From: Trina

Subject: Obsessed with Twilight

Hi Kimberly,

I've read the entire series and the first book, *Twilight*, twice. I was spellbound with this series…. The feelings that I have for these characters are unexplainable. No one knows the obsession I have over these books.

The draw. There's the average girl, Bella: popular, beautiful, and talented. There's a beautiful and perfect boy, Edward: extremely handsome, infamous, talented, but intimidating, smart, not friendly.

The story. Boy and girl see each other. Girl is drawn to him by his looks. Boy is drawn to her by his instinct (her blood/his thirst). Boy is also drawn because of curiosity. She is "different"—he can't read her thoughts. Boy struggles against his natural instincts with such intensity he has to flee.

Edward is a NOBLE character. He resists his nature because of the love he has for his family. It would cause them problems, and he knew he would be a disappointment to them. And also as he gets to know Bella he starts to value her life more than his own selfish desires.

Edward falls in love with this average girl, but to him, Bella is extraordinary. He sees her soul and loves it. He does indeed see her physical beauty when she can't. Edward sees her as the most beautiful girl in the world. He has never been so enthralled by someone. He is amazed at his own feelings for her. He finds the feelings confusing and dangerous and exciting.

Through hours of talking, he starts to trust her and reveals his secret. He opens up completely, and it's a big risk to his whole family. TRUST becomes a huge issue for both of them.

He PROTECTS her at all costs, even at the price of revealing his secret.

He becomes VULNERABLE. Sex doesn't seem to be an issue because his natural instincts are not the same as other boys'. Edward's lust is for blood, Bella's in particular. But as he discovers more of who she is, he learns to control that lust and puts her best interest before his own.

He becomes SELFLESS. He feels that her very existence is more vital than his desires. Edward knows that allowing Bella near him is extremely dangerous, life threatening. So he lets her in on all the details of what a vampire is. He is hoping all the while that it will be too frightening and bizarre for her.

He lets her make the CHOICE. If she leaves, it will break his heart, but he knows it will be for the best and he will not pursue her. He loves her that much. This is a SACRIFICIAL type of love.

Bella makes her choice to stay. She loves him so much that she wants to spend eternity with him—meaning she would have to become what he is, a vampire.

Edward refuses. He will settle for a short time with her until her natural death, just to be able to be with her. There is the SACRIFICE again.

Look again at these qualities: Trust. Protection. Selflessness. Choice. Vulnerability. Sacrifice. Love.

Who doesn't want this in a boyfriend? The perfect guy with incredible looks and talent to boot! Perfection (except for the vampire part). He is still flawed because he battles with right versus wrong and temptation and guilt and lust.

By the time I reached the end of these books and she finally is changed into a vampire (in order to save her life) I found myself thinking, *Wow, finally, now they can be happy and have their happily ever after.*

I loved Trina's honesty. Through her email, I saw the books and film from her perspective and started to think about a few things myself.

So why do we devour these books whole and memorize quotes from the films? Perhaps it comes down to two main reasons:

✝ "The feelings that I have for these characters are unexplainable. No one knows the obsession I have over these books."—Trina ✝

1. The love story between Bella and Edward is captivating.

2. We desire our own epic love story in real time.

Just breathe …

What do you think it is about Bella and Edward's story that draws so many to the books and film? What do you love or not love about it?

Let's take a close look at Edward. I have to admit, he seems like the full package: charming, attentive, noble, and mysterious. His devotion is evident in the way he talks to Bella, how carefully he protects her. He even watches over her as she sleeps! And his desire to really know her is flattering. He wants to figure her out.

An article in *Vanity Fair* characterizes Edward this way: "Everything a girl could want in one dreamy envelope, Edward is the answer to a princess's prayers—doting, fiercely protective, carrying his

✛ So why do we devour these books whole and memorize quotes from the films? ✛

beloved great distances in his arms like a groom forever crossing the honeymoon threshold."[8]

We are enthralled by the idea of our very own Edward. Is this fascination because he is a vampire? No. We are drawn to him because of the many awesome qualities he possesses. Let's look at those qualities again: Trust. Protection. Selflessness. Choice. Vulnerability. Sacrifice. Love. With Edward, Bella is desired. Protected. Loved and fought for. It's obvious in his continual attentiveness to her every thought, his desire to understand who she is. To receive this kind of attention from a mystifying, handsome, talented, intelligent guy—and to have that guy so interested in every detail of what she considers an otherwise boring life—would be enough to enrapture any vulnerable heart. If we're being honest, it's the connection we all long for.

But there's more to it than just connection. The fact that he is a vampire makes things *exciting*. A popular blog recently posed the question, "What is it about a vampire hero that is so irresistible and sexy?" One reader left this revealing comment: "It's got to be that irresistible combination of Alpha-ness and possessiveness

… of course all mixed in with a huge dose of deep internal tor-
ture." Edward's untouchable, "forbidden territory" vampire self
is attractive. But Edward calls *himself* a killer and a monster. He
knows his tendencies and attraction to Bella are dangerous.

But lots of girls have told me that they admire many qualities
of Edward's character. He is from a family of "good" vampires
who control their thirst for human blood. He is chaste and self-
controlled. He continually holds himself back from getting too
physically close to Bella. It is not the vampire's passion that is
captivating but his self-control. Ken
Gelder has said that "there is that
sense that because Edward is such a
self-restraining vampire, he's not really
a vampire."[10]

> Jennie Yabroff of *Newsweek* writes, "These vampires are not so much scary as noble, fighting against their inherent natures for the sake of love."[9]

In other words, maybe Edward can't help who he is, but he
can control what he does and doesn't allow himself to do. It's an
admirable example of self-restraint. We girls love that, don't we?

And then there's Bella, the girl next door. She's clumsy and self-
mocking. Not totally insecure, but not wildly popular either. I think
we can all relate to her in one way or another.

"It doesn't surprise me that girls identify with Bella, a character
that cannot imagine she is lovable," writes Beth Felker Jones, an
assistant professor of theology at Wheaton College. "Her clumsi-
ness and willingness to erase herself form an apt portrayal of the
self-understanding of many young women today. Dark romance, a
love that erases the awkward heroine, is an answer to desire and self-
loathing that draws on the worst cultural assumptions about what it
means to be female."[11]

Just breathe ...

If you have seen or read *Twilight*, how would you describe Bella? (For instance, clumsy, brave, normal.) Did you find yourself relating to her character at all? If so, how?

SOMETHING MORE

Looking back on the notes I took while researching vampires, I see one thing very clearly. At some point in the late twentieth century, the vampire's persona became a "gray area." By that, I mean he was no longer considered altogether bad. Oh, vampires were still "bad boys"—but it was *cool* to like them. Maybe you'll agree with what Diane Robina, president of the cable horror channel FEARnet, said: "Vampires are the new rock stars. They are the bad boys your parents don't want you to date."[12]

> ✝ "Vampires are the new rock stars. They are the bad boys your parents don't want you to date." —Diane Robina ✝

It's a truly interesting transformation. Is it just an example of literary creativity, or could it be just another blurred line between good and evil? It does seem that we're having a harder time telling right from wrong, truth from lies these days. You don't always know who the villain is when he enters the room. And vampires? Hey, they might even be the heroes.

So what do we do with all of this? It's clear that we are so drawn to this story and others like it. Despite the fact—or maybe because of the fact—that Edward is mysterious and dangerous, we're almost irresistibly swept up in the adventurous romance. We so desperately want to experience such a story ourselves. But then the credits roll or the last page is turned, and we're back in our own reality. Our lives are just the same as they've always been. There are no good vampires—or even vampires of any kind—and Edward remains that character in our head.

Have you felt this way? Like you wished you could really live in Bella and Edward's world and leave your own behind? It makes me start to wonder if there's actually something more going on here, a deeper reason that we're all so attracted to and drawn into this story.

Here are some of the comments I've heard from girls who love *Twilight:*

〜 "I *cried.* I kept thinking, oh my gosh, is this guy for real? He's not like other guys."

〜 "Edward is way hot … sooo cute!"

〜 "I liked the romance.… I wish a guy could be that way with me."

〜 "Maybe what I liked was the fact that they're not supposed to be together but they are."

〜 "He's into what is best for her … well, most of the time."

Just breathe …

God thinks that your reality is way more interesting than Edward and Bella's. Think of at least three things about your own life that you are proud of. Maybe it's people in your life or the way you can make someone smile … or maybe something unique that makes you uniquely *you.*

Recently, I was talking with a group of girls after a conference. Their faces lit up when I mentioned *Twilight.* One of them told me that she couldn't stop thinking about the movie. *Twilight* was her obsession. She began sharing quote after quote. Soon the whole group joined in—how many lines could they remember? I could see that they were reliving the adventure together. You could hear it in their voices and see it in the excitement on their faces.

Then I asked them about *their* lives. Who was their true hero? Who offered them the love, protection, and unending relationship filled with hope and life they were desperate for? That totally stumped them; they didn't have an answer. So then we talked about how no mortal can unconditionally fulfill these things. A few may come close, but no one offers perfection. No one offers love without a price. So why do our hearts keep longing so hard after something we can never find—something that simply does not exist?

Unless it does. Unless this longing is a hunger for what our souls were created for.

What if our hearts were created to long for this love because it is actually out there longing for us? What if our souls were shaped for Someone? Someone amazing, who is incredibly attentive to our every need and will treat us better than we could ever imagine. Someone always present in our lives who experiences life with us.

You can see the charm of Edward and all he is for Bella. Imagine having that type of relationship connection in your life.

For some, this may be a radical thought to wrap your mind around—but imagine that this iconic, hunky, bad-boy hero Edward could be outdone so easily by an eternally loving, fiercely protective Savior. Pretty cool thought.

This fascination with Edward and the draw he has with so many is just a shadow of the true epic love story offered by our true Immortal Hero, the Savior of the world, *Jesus Christ!*

"What if I'm not the hero? What if I'm the bad guy?"

"If you're smart ... you'll stay away from me."

"So the lion fell in love with the lamb."

"He looks at you like you're something to eat."

"Bella, you are my life now."

"I don't have the strength to stay away from you anymore."

"Everything about me invites you in."

"Then don't."

"I dream about being with you forever."

"Is it not enough just to have a long and happy life with me?"

Jesus offered His life to provide life forever with Him.

> He reached down from heaven and rescued me;
> he drew me out of deep waters. He rescued me
> from my powerful enemies, from those who hated
> me and were too strong for me. They attacked
> me at a moment when I was in distress, but the
> LORD supported me. He led me to a place of
> safety; he rescued me because he delights in me.
>
> *(Ps. 18:16–19 NLT)*

In *Teen Vogue*, Kristen Stewart, the actress who plays Bella, describes the movie like this: "It's about what drives you to love."[13]

To be respected and intensely loved is to have someone who is forever loyal and unselfishly true to your heart. Think about that one. When you experience this type of undying love … nothing else compares.

Just breathe …

Oh, I hope you know the amazing love of your true Hero! How does having this kind of love change your life? Not sure? Stay with me.…

Relationship with a guy like Edward:	Relationship with Christ, your true Immortal Hero:
Offers excitement for the moment	Christ provides never-ending adventure and life-giving purpose (Lamentations 3:22–23)
Seems intriguing/ mysterious	Christ is a mystery—eternal treasures are hidden in Him (Colossians 2:2–3)
Offers protection/a sense of security for the moment	Provides unending security, certainty, and strength (2 Corinthians 12:10)
Offers a love that sweeps you off your feet	Provides unconditional, unfailing love that endures forever (Psalm 136)

What others can you think of?

CHAPTER 2

Charmed in the Garden

Now the serpent was more crafty than
any of the wild animals the LORD God
had made. He said to the woman,
"Did God really say, 'You must not
eat from any tree in the garden'?"

(Gen. 3:1 NIV)

The hiss. Eve had heard that sound before.

This time the *Sssssssss* was intermingled with words, each sound flowing smoothly into the next, like a piece of music. She listened carefully, intrigued by the beautiful, haunting melody.

Eve wasn't sure what to expect in this forbidden territory. She turned slowly in the direction of the chilling sound, craning her neck to locate the object of her curiosity.

And then she saw him.

The Serpent. Coiled in a slinky pyramid on the branch of a gorgeous tree—the only tree in the garden that God had warned Adam and Eve not to eat from.

Eve approached slowly and cautiously and spoke in a whisper, "What are you doing here?" She might as well have asked herself the same question. *Why was she standing in the one forbidden spot in the garden?*

The Serpent seemed pleased by her presence. He wrapped himself around a branch, then began slithering toward her. As he drew closer, Eve involuntarily took a step forward. She felt uneasy but deeply intrigued. There was something hypnotic about this creature.

Keeping her eyes on the Serpent as he slithered farther up into the branches, she wondered why he seemed so perfectly at ease in such a place. "Do you come here often—to this tree?" she asked. And she wondered, *Doesn't he know the Creator's rule?*

Lost in thought and waiting for his reply, Eve took a good look at the Tree of the Knowledge of Good and Evil, as God called it. She watched the Serpent move closer and closer to the dangling fruit hanging from the limbs of the enormous tree. Suddenly, Adam's descriptions of this fruit flooded her mind. He had found his way here more than once and had given countless descriptions of this magnificent tree, its ravishing fruit and shining leaves and the way the bark caught and held the afternoon sunlight.

Eve suddenly noticed that a single glistening piece of fruit hung just within her reach. It was perfectly ripe and looked as though it was bursting with flavor. The longer she gazed at it, the more enticing it became.

The Serpent spoke again, softly, interrupting her thoughts. His words gently coaxed her to move closer, just to take a better look at the fruit. His voice was unbearably soft and his words intrigued her. *What would it hurt just to look?*

In that fateful moment, doubt about her beloved Creator God crept in.

Captured by the intrigue of the forbidden and caught up in the thrill of discovery, Eve's heart was deceived. As they bantered about whether God really meant *this* tree, if He had actually said she would *die,* Eve became an invited victim of the Serpent.

As Eve finally reached for the fruit, she discovered it wasn't as difficult as she had anticipated. Touching what was forbidden gave way to unfamiliar feelings within her. Holding it brought an unsettling mix of fear and tantalizing excitement. She must share this fruit with Adam!

Expecting delight from their shared meal, Eve turned to find Adam's haunted eyes meet her own. His look made Eve's heart and mind race. *What have I done?*

It was too late. Eve could feel her heart throbbing as questions flew through her mind. Where was the Serpent? Why had she trusted his words? What would this mean when God found out? Why was Adam looking at her with such distaste?

She felt terribly afraid … and completely alone.

Just breathe …

If we were sitting at Starbucks talking, first of all I'd buy your coffee or chai. Then I'd love to hear about you. What would you say are the hardest temptations that you are forced to debate in your mind? What is your "forbidden fruit choice" that can so often appear beautiful and perfect?

THE ULTIMATE VAMPIRE

Have you ever felt like Eve, tempted to taste the forbidden fruit and then devastated by the consequences? The garden of Eden was home to humanity's first encounter with sin. The stage was set with a cast of characters that can be found in virtually every great story that's been written since. Looking back at this historical event, we see that the villain, Satan, is the same Enemy you and I face today. And what a villain! It can be difficult to picture him, but this devious character is very real, and he despises the Truth.

The Bible calls Satan a snake, dragon, tempter, and ruler of darkness. Throughout this book, I'll refer to him as the "Ultimate Vampire." Does that comparison surprise you? Keep reading, and I believe you'll come to see several reasons I've come to think of him like this.

> Stephenie Meyer chose the *Twilight* cover of the forbidden fruit for a reason. From her Web site: "The apple on the cover of Twilight represents 'forbidden fruit.' I used the scripture from Genesis (located just after the table of contents) because I loved the phrase 'the fruit of the knowledge of good and evil.' Isn't this exactly what Bella ends up with? … To me it says: *choice.*"[1]

ILLUSIONS OF ESCAPE

Many of you already know that Satan, the Ultimate Vampire, is a master schemer who draws you in to trap you. His lies and motives are based on his selfish, twisted desire for your deep disappointment and, ultimately, your destruction.

But it's what you don't know about this Vampire that makes him so dangerous. The thing is, sometimes he really doesn't seem so bad. Just like he did with Eve in the garden, this Vampire has figured out how to disguise himself so you don't automatically recognize him. Pretty sneaky, isn't he? This is why Ephesians 6:11 tells us, "Put on the whole armor of God, that you may be able to stand against the schemes of the devil" (ESV). He has schemes you can't even imagine, and they are targeted directly at your life.

The character James in *Twilight,* a merciless tracker vampire, gives us a bit of a picture of the Ultimate Vampire. He can appear to be beautiful and pleasant when he needs to be, but in reality he is devious and tricky, out for blood and for destruction, prowling around, tracking his prey in order to devour them. Remember Edward's statement to Bella when he's explaining vampires to her? "I'm the world's most dangerous predator. Everything about me invites you in. My voice, my face, even my smell. As if I would need any of that. As if you could outrun me. As if you could fight me off. I'm designed to kill."

> ✝ Satan ... is a master schemer who draws you in to trap you. His lies and motives are based on his selfish, twisted desire for your deep disappointment and, ultimately, your destruction. ✝

Edward also told Bella that James wouldn't stop once he had her in his sight. And James is not intent just on killing Bella but on making her suffer horribly for her loved ones to watch ... *shudder!*

And believe it or not, your Enemy, Satan, the Ultimate Vampire, is worse than James—he doesn't just want to destroy our mortal lives; he desires our immortal lives as well.

Let's look at how the Bible talks about the Ultimate Vampire.

1. He is the worst kind of liar. Think about it. The Bible describes him this way: "He was a murderer from the beginning, and

has nothing to do with the truth, because there is no truth in him. When he lies, he speaks out of his own character, for he is a liar and the father of lies" (John 8:44 ESV).

Like vampires you read about in novels (and may see in TV series and movies like *True Blood* and *Interview with a Vampire*), Satan uses alluring enticements to trick you into trusting him and compromising your convictions. His goal is for you to let down your guard so you'll eventually give in to his agenda.

2. His plan is to entrap his victims and suck the life from them. Eve found this out when she allowed herself to come closer to the Serpent and carry on a conversation. This interaction ultimately led her to believe she had misunderstood God and deserved to do whatever she wanted. Do you see the battle?

Look what God has to say about this: "But I am afraid that as the serpent deceived Eve by his cunning, your thoughts will be led astray from a sincere and pure devotion to Christ" (2 Cor. 11:3 ESV). The goal of this Vampire is to drain away the lifeblood of a vibrant life and a close relationship with Christ.

3. He can look attractive, but he represents death. The Ultimate Vampire shows up in many forms, speaking words that often sound promising and encourage you to draw near. But things that look so harmless—if not measured carefully against God's Word—often lead to sin and painful consequences. "Satan himself masquerades as an angel of light" (2 Cor. 11:14 NIV), but he is really the ruler of darkness (Eph. 6:12).

The good news is that if you've accepted Christ as your Savior and Hero, Satan cannot ultimately succeed. He can tempt us, leading us into traps and enticements that can harm us, but he cannot have us eternally. When we belong to Christ—the Immortal Hero—we are rescued. We are safe.

KEISHA'S STORY

The work of the Vampire was evident in the life of Keisha, a teen I met after a conference in Atlanta. Keisha thought she had found the perfect guy when she started dating Derek. Besides having an incredible body and adorable smile, Derek made Keisha laugh—something she needed to help her forget life at home. Her dad had abandoned the family for another woman when she was just a baby, and her mom's current boyfriend often abused Keisha when her mom was at work.

The escape Derek offered Keisha seemed so nice at first. When she was with him she'd forget all the pain she carried—at least for a while. But that all crumbled as she came to realize Derek had certain "habits," things she later wished she could erase from her memory: drinking, drugs, and how Derek treated her when he was high. But she also loved his attention.

Keisha came to understand that there were two different Dereks: the one doing stuff that made him crazy and the sweet guy he could sometimes be with her. She wanted to believe the sweet guy was Derek's true self—that if she'd just wait for him, he could be that funny, cute guy again.

But Derek didn't change. Things only grew worse when, in a desperate attempt to be close to Derek and remain a part of his life, Keisha started doing everything he was into.

Keisha found herself in that trapped place through her own choices, but the work of the Vampire was evident. Derek didn't *appear* to be a bad choice … at first. And much of the time, the Vampire's enticements don't appear to be evil because his lies and deception are well camouflaged.

Finally, one day Keisha had had enough. But the question was … how to escape? She was lonely and hurting. She also needed to escape what had become a dangerous home life.

This place of desperation is the perfect scenario for the Ultimate Vampire. Here is how he works: He sets you up for further disappointment, offering enticements specially targeted at your weakness. He knows what you want and what situation will draw you in.

In Keisha's case, she was looking for a new relationship that would offer the love she so needed. In walked Brett, the perfect distraction. But her relationship with him ultimately led to more pain and further hurtful conse-quences, and she's still caught in the midst of regret and disillusions.

✛ He sets you up for further disappointment, offering enticements specially targeted at your weakness. He knows what you want and what situation will draw you in. ✛

Just breathe …

If you could talk with my friend Keisha today, what would you tell her? How do you help someone who feels so far away from any hope at all?

Make no mistake: The Vampire's goal is for your life to be shattered. He wants you disillusioned—filled with confusion and sadness. He offers temptations that are tailored to your life, playing on both your strengths and weaknesses.

The story of your life is interwoven with the temptations offered by the Vampire and the subsequent choices you make. Just like Eve, you and I are confronted every day with situations that force us to decide: *What will I choose?*

There are millions of choices facing us throughout the story of our lives. As you live out your story, you'll discover that each decision brings either blessing or pain. Eve's story shows the painful consequences of sin, but it also reveals the great gift of the Hero's forgiveness. Continue reading through verse 21 of Genesis chapter 3, and you'll see how God provided graciously and lovingly for Adam and Eve. Even though He was deeply hurt by their choice, God made garments out of animal skins so they would no longer be naked.

Something had to die for those coverings to be made. You see, before Adam and Eve sinned, there was no such thing as death; life in the garden was perfection like we'll never know on this earth. But then they broke trust with God. They must have felt hopeless in their sin, separated from the relationship they had enjoyed with God. What they didn't realize was that God already had a plan—He would send His Son to die as the ultimate sacrifice. He would offer rescue!

I've talked to hundreds of girls who, like Eve, feel hopeless and filled with despair, without thought of a possible rescue. Maybe this is where you find yourself as well. The Vampire wants us to stay there in that place of fear, paralyzed by our scars of pain and regret. Hearing these true stories fills me with anger toward the Enemy of our souls and makes me wonder, *How can I help girls see that the True Hero can set them free?*

TRAPPED IN THE DARK

Carrie stood before me, holding her belly, tears streaming down her face. She finally spoke: She had beaten her own body in order to have a miscarriage. The scars would tell her story, but she'd been harboring this dark secret for months.

She never would have imagined that this would be her story. Carrie was raised in a Christian home by parents who loved God and had prayed over her since she was born. Anxious to explore life beyond her parents' watchful eyes, she drifted from the standard she had been raised to uphold.

Maintaining a secret life was exhausting, and the web of lies grew thick. Then she found herself pregnant and unsure who the father of her baby was. Carrie panicked. Ashamed and afraid, she believed the Vampire's lie that no one would understand—that no one could help her now.

Carrie was desperate for answers as she told me about the pain she still carried inside. Could she ever forgive herself for what she'd done? How could she live beyond her horrible memories?

I shared hope with Carrie that day. I want you to know that same hope.

As a conference speaker, I've had many conversations with girls who've experienced difficult things: being in hurtful relationships, fighting addictions to drugs, drinking, cutting their bodies, starving themselves, hating themselves, wanting to end their lives. Some share about wanting out of their secret lives but not knowing how to escape. Some share about family struggles. Others struggle with thinking they don't measure up.

Maybe, like Keisha, you have a broken heart. Maybe you have

a scarred body like Carrie. Whatever your situation, my guess is that in some way you feel shame, hurt, or abandonment.

Different lives, different stories. The common thread is that every young woman hurts somewhere deep inside. We long to be loved and desired, fought for and protected. But often that dream seems distant, like a cruel joke.

Where is the hope?

THE ULTIMATE HERO

Every great story has a hero. Someone who saves the day. Someone who loves the girl who feels unlovable. Someone who offers strength and stability for a family, a community, a nation. Someone who chooses to save the lives of others over his own. A hero is strong— sometimes wise, sometimes handsome, and always brave.

I'm here to tell you that there is a True Hero, and He sees your pain and struggles. He fiercely protects and faithfully loves you. He doesn't draw you in to abandon you; instead, He pulls you through the struggles and dark times you find yourself facing. He laid down His life willingly for yours. He offers constant protection and a life full of peace, hope, forgiveness, and lasting love.

> ✝ "God is faithful; he will not let you be tempted beyond what you can bear. But when you are tempted, he will also provide a way out so that you can stand up under it" (1 Cor. 10:13 NIV). ✝

He promises to help you out of any dark place if you'll turn to Him. This is what the apostle Paul said about Him: "God is faithful; he will not let you be tempted beyond what you can bear. But when you are tempted, he will also provide a way out so that you can stand up under it" (1 Cor. 10:13 NIV).

When you find yourself in desperate need of a rescuer, *He*—your Savior and Lord, Jesus Christ—provides a way out. You may not be able to eliminate the struggles, but you can hold tightly to Him. In other words, He offers escape.

YOU HAVE A STORY

Just like Eve, Keisha, and Carrie, you have a story. And within that story are many chapters. I wish I could sit with you and listen to some of those chapters! I would love to hear about the wonderful things you've experienced. I would also love to comfort you as you share about the painful hurts you carry so bravely.

Whenever I talk to girls, I have the honor of hearing their stories. Sometimes we laugh, sometimes we cry. But I'll tell you this: Girls have shared more stories with me about feeling lonely and abandoned than anything else. Together we've asked God for wisdom, for healing, for His love to cover us. And He has met us there.

I believe He wants to meet with you, too. So I'll sit with you, too, okay? I'll hold your hand and pray for you as we walk through the pages of this book together. In fact, as I write these words, I'm praying over you. I want you to know the hope that is yours through Christ— *your Hero*. He is with you. He wants to comfort you with His love.

Just breathe …

What's your story? If there are important pieces of it that you've never shared with anyone, I'd like to encourage you to do that with a trusted friend, parent, or youth worker.

My friend, perhaps you feel there's just no way out this time. Maybe you question God's forgiveness and belief in your future. If you feel trapped by the Vampire's schemes and enticements and have no desire to move forward … *please hold on!* In your weakest moment, that's often when you'll get a glimpse of your need for the Ultimate Hero to rescue you. At the end of hope, God's love and grace can find you.

When you're ready, your Ultimate Hero is there—loving, strong, and sure. He will hear your heart. He will listen, walk with you, carry you. Let's find out what He offers. In the pages to come, I'll introduce you to a Hero who is true and honorable and desires to protect your honor with His own.

> "The LORD your God is with you, he is
> mighty to save. He will take great delight
> in you, he will quiet you with his love, he
> will rejoice over you with singing"
> *(Zeph. 3:17 NIV).*

Just breathe …

What is going through your head when I say that you have a True Hero, someone better than "any Edward out there," who will never leave you? Do you think that this is possible? What do you want Him to rescue you from?

CHAPTER 3

Poison in the Bite

I do not understand what I do.... I know
that nothing good lives in me, that is, in my
sinful nature. For I have the desire to do what
is good, but I cannot carry it out. For what I
do is not the good I want to do; no, the evil
I do not want to do—this I keep on doing.

(Rom. 7:15, 18–19 NIV)

Think back to the seemingly innocent offer Eve accepted in the garden. The deceiving Ultimate Vampire devised his schemes in such a way as to lure her in. He captivated her with his venomous lies in order to claim her as his victim ... and then she was trapped.

Imagine being the first woman ever to choose sin and experience guilt. Never before had a human stepped away from God. What a scary moment! Eve wasn't thinking about the consequences. She was thinking "in the moment." She chose to believe the lie.

It's what Eve didn't know about this Ultimate Vampire that made him seem not so bad to her. He disguised himself in such a way that he didn't seem scary at all. Satan encouraged Eve to doubt God's own words to her. Look at Genesis 3:1: "Now the serpent was more crafty than any of the wild animals the LORD God had made. He said to the woman, 'Did God really say, "You must not eat from any tree in the garden"?'" (NIV).

Think about the way his words caught her off guard. He went right for her thoughts and targeted her relationship with God. Doubting God's words led Eve to turn away from God and make a choice that went against His commands. A sneaky deception led to very painful consequences.

The Vampire's carefully worded deception was in some way desirable to her. She trusted his words, and they eventually brought death. She lost her home—the security of the garden. For the first time in her life, Eve faced feelings of loss, loneliness, guilt, shame.

She lost immortality; her life was given a limit.

THE BATTLE WITHIN

The Ultimate Vampire is the conniving accuser who offers enticements carefully targeted to our lives—with our strengths and weaknesses in mind. He feeds us many lies that we accept hook, line, and sinker. When we are in the midst of these battles, in way over our heads, our weaknesses are used against us.

There's an unseen battle going on in your life, for your affections and for your heart. It's like a game to the Vampire as he figures out our weaknesses and works us into his plot.

Think about how in *Twilight*, James, the merciless tracker vampire, threatens Bella's life. Edward shields her, and she escapes only to have James follow her. Then the hunt begins. James leads Bella to

POISON IN THE BITE

believe she can save the life of her mom by sacrificing her own. Bella says, "Surely it was a good way to die, in the place of someone else, someone I loved. Noble, even."

But she wasn't saving her mother's life. The evil tracker vampire took Bella's loyalty and love for her mother and used it against her.

If this doesn't sound familiar, it should. Like I said before, the Ultimate Vampire's lies and motives are based on his selfish, twisted desire for your destruction and your deep disappointment. He uses the same deceptive techniques to work his plan into our lives today.

> ✛ "Surely it was a good way to die, in the place of someone else, someone I loved. Noble, even."—Bella ✛

THE DISGUISE OF EVIL

There's a pattern here that we need to recognize. The Vampire devises plans to hit you where you are painfully weak. Lies that look innocent will lure you into his trap. He targets your emotions so that you feel incapable, insecure, and desperate. He does this to create in you a false sense of desperation. If his plan is successfully executed, you fall into his plot and land as his victim. All the while he remains carefully disguised and often undetected.

Here's how the Ultimate Vampire's plan works:

1. *The Struggle.* I buy into the lie ("venom") that brings paralysis and destruction.

The lies are evil and dark, but at first they won't appear to be. They often seem so innocent.

His lies and deception are well camouflaged, and we are often trapped into believing them.

2. *The Substitute*. I compromise and accept the intriguing entice-ments offered to ease the pain.

Example of substitutes include cutting, sexual relationships, sub-stance abuse, anorexia/bulimia, homosexuality, and suicide. Instead of easing the pain, they result in deeper emptiness, pain, and dis-satisfaction with our lives.

3. *The Serum*. I receive the truth of God's Word.

The Ultimate Vampire's lie is contrasted with God's truth, expos-ing it for what it is. This ultimately brings strength and healing.

I hope that is as eye-opening for you as it is for me. We can know these things in our heads for our entire lives: the Enemy's lies that deceive, our tendency to compromise, and God's truth that brings freedom from deception. But until we see it play out in real time, we keep playing the same games. I'm over the Vampire's lies—how about you?

Just think about the patterns of lies that come at you fast and furious. Ever feel absolutely alone and unloved? Your loneliness and insecurity play right into his hand.

How about feeling unworthy of love or forgiveness? Your doubt about yourself, and the shame you carry, blinds you to the Truth.

Maybe you're caught up in a relationship gone terribly wrong. Or maybe you're locked in crazy habits that have you entangled. You're filled with fear, questioning everything inside. Where does that leave you? Captured.

BATTLEFIELD OF THE MIND

Sometimes the messages we receive pull us in two different direc-tions. It's that inner debate about what we should do versus what we want to do. Each voice conflicts with the other. The hard part is deciding which to follow. Ever been there?

Paul talks about this exact struggle in Romans: "I do not understand what I do.... I know that nothing good lives in me, that is, in my sinful nature. For I have the desire to do what is good, but I cannot carry it out. For what I do is not the good I want to do; no, the evil I do not want to do—this I keep on doing" (7:15, 18–19 NIV).

Sounds a little confusing, doesn't it? When you stop and think about it, though, it makes sense. We will continue to struggle in our choices, but God wants to help us work through our struggles by giving us His truths. His Word offers direction.

I've heard it said that your conscience is a text message of truth your head gets from God. I love that! We receive those messages of truth inside, urging us to follow Him. But we also receive thousands of deceptive messages that pull us in different directions.

> ✛ We will continue to struggle in our choices, but God wants to help us work through our struggles by giving us His truths. His Word offers direction. ✛

These deceptive thoughts can't be from God because His words are true to Himself—and He is your gracious, loving Creator. We need to know how to distinguish what words are from God and what words are not.

ENTRAPMENT OF LIES

My favorite part about speaking to thousands of girls across the country is spending hours together afterward. It's during those times that I hear about many difficult struggles girls are battling.

After hundreds of conversations with girls over the years, I have come up with a list of the top life-sucking lies I see consuming girls today. Let's take a look at the most prominent lies I've seen tear away at girls' hearts and lives; maybe you'll relate to a few. We'll also explore how to recognize and break free from the lies.

No matter what areas trip you up the most, you'll see how you can face the lie behind your struggle and connect with God's truths. That's when you can be free! It comes down to simple trust. Will you accept God's words that lead to life and freedom, or will you choose to believe the Vampire's lies that bring death and defeat?

✝ It comes down to simple trust. Will you accept God's words that lead to life and freedom, or will you choose to believe the Vampire's lies that bring death and defeat? ✝

LIE #1: "I AM NOT BEAUTIFUL."

The Struggle

Look closely at one of the lies our society tries to sell: "You must be physically perfect in order to be accepted, in order to feel truly beautiful." Believing you must have a certain look—a toned body, a certain color of skin, commercial-worthy hair, or perfectly straight teeth—in order to be beautiful is such a lie. But it is also easily bought into. What you take in from the media and from social expectations feeds the lie.

Remember how throughout the *Twilight* books Bella struggles with her view of herself? I know many of us can identify with her on this one. In spite of

"A recent study by the Dove Campaign for Real Beauty revealed that nine out of every ten girls want to change at least one aspect of their appearance, and only 2 percent of women around the world would describe themselves as beautiful."[1]

Your heavenly Father speaks His truths over your life. "The [K]ing is enthralled by your beauty, [say your name here]; honor him, [say your name again], for he is your [L]ord" (Ps. 45:11 NIV). You are valued and treasured, thought of constantly by God as His child! Remember, you are accepted completely—just as you are!

how often Edward tells her she's beautiful and that he loves her, she continues to doubt him—she can't seem to take his words to heart, no matter how true they are. At the prom, she feels ridiculous and uncomfortable, even though she's gorgeous. And even on her wedding day, she's comparing her beauty to Rosalie!

Just breathe …

How many times do you find yourself unhappy with "you"? How do you normally respond? Shopping … coffee … movies … maybe pushing yourself with a busy schedule? Want to know what you can do that lasts a lot longer than any of those "quick fixes"? Stay with me.…

Do you ever find yourself struggling with this absolute LIE of a "perfect" image? You may not even realize you're accepting it inside. Here's one message this ugly lie might be saying to you: "If you are physically perfect, then you are beautiful; if you are beautiful, then you are loved." Pretty sad, isn't it?

The Rescue

In the midst of these ugly lies, God offers His words of truth.

> The [K]ing is enthralled by your beauty;
> honor him, for he is your [L]ord.
> *(Ps. 45:11 NIV)*

He restates the truth: YOU ARE BEAUTIFUL. God's focus is very different, isn't it? He's already said you are beautiful to Him, and He can't lie. It's impossible.

You may be thinking, *How can words, even God's words, change what I think about myself?* But when you're hearing God's words, you can be assured of the power and change they bring … because of who is speaking them.

Is it hard for you to believe that anyone would think you are truly beautiful? Let God's words of Truth counter what's in your head.

LIE #2: "I HAVE TO PROVE MY LOVE IN ORDER TO BE LOVED."

The Struggle

Here's another lie many girls buy into: You need to have sex in order for him to accept you.

Let's take a closer look at what this lie is really saying. It promises that by giving away your body, you receive worth—no matter the cost. What a blatant lie!

What is sacrificed here often brings pain and comes with a high price. You're not just offering your body; you're giving away a sacred part of you. You may think you can escape the pain and consequences with a particular guy or relationship because it seems so great, but God's words of protection over your heart and body say otherwise:

> Keep far away from sexual sins. All the
> other sins a person commits are outside
> his body. But sexual sins are sins against

one's own body. Don't you know that your
bodies are temples of the Holy Spirit? The
Spirit is in you. You have received him
from God. You do not belong to yourselves.
Christ has paid the price for you. So use
your bodies in a way that honors God.

(1 Cor. 6:18–20 NIrV)

The Rescue

So what is God saying about this? Let's go back to the fact that
God doesn't just love the surface of you. Remember, His love and
commitment to you go so much deeper.

Think about this. Do you *have* to
give away your body to be beautiful or
valued by someone? This lie can be so
easy to believe.

Giving such a gift doesn't make you
a beautiful person. In fact, it leaves you
feeling empty and dissatisfied. It doesn't
prove your value. You are worthy of so
much more.

"A CDC study estimates
that one in four (26 percent)
young women between the
ages of 14 and 19 in the
United States—or 3.2 milllion
teenage girls—is infected
with at least one of the most
common sexually transmitted
diseases (human papil-
lomavirus [HPV], chlamydia,
herpes simplex virus, and
trichomoniasis)."[2]

I've cried with many, many teens
who have poured out their hearts to me about this lie. I've heard
them say over and over again, "If I could just go back and do things
differently ..." Still others have been hurt by someone else believing
the lie. Gretta is one of them.

Gretta, a beautiful newlywed, confided in me about her struggle
to accept and forgive her husband's past. Gretta had carefully guarded

her relationships and had remained a virgin until her wedding day. Her husband had not. His college years were filled with things he now considered with regret.

Did she love him? Absolutely. But she struggled with letting go and moving on. She shared, "This was devastating to me, and we both cried over it a lot. He'd change it all if he could, I know. But we did have to wrestle through that, and it was tough. Imagining him with another woman that way made me want to vomit, and we each needed God to heal our hearts for stuff he did in the past." Our choices today really can affect our lives in the future. By choosing to be sexually involved, you are sinning against your own body; you are hurting *yourself* and potentially someone else as well.

When we find ourselves needing His forgiveness, we find Him to be faithful. God treasures your life. Your body, soul, and mind. You are His beautiful creation—no matter what!

✛ God treasures your life. Your body, soul, and mind. You are His beautiful creation—no matter what! ✛

The unconditional forgiveness God offers was the forgiveness both Gretta and her husband needed to cling to. Gretta had to give God her thoughts and her hurt … and she did. They both did, and God strengthened their relationship through this struggle.

If you've believed this lie, I'm asking God to help you accept His love that reaches past your mistakes. I'm asking Him to assure you of new beginnings He has for you.

LIE #3: "I AM WORTHLESS."

The Struggle

Let's check out the thinking behind this huge, awful lie: "You are not worth anyone's time, interest, or love; and just like everyone else, God doesn't have the love you're looking for." The fact is, if the people who are really important to you don't give you time or take interest in your life, you may begin to believe the same about God.

We each have a deep desire inside to be loved and accepted. The Ultimate Vampire knows that, and he makes this lie seem believable. But God's love—His total acceptance—is what you're searching for. You don't have to buy into the lies, like Gina did.

Gina felt invisible. Her deep struggle was inside. There weren't very many who knew the details of the pain she carried. It all began when her friends in preschool would laugh and call her fat and ugly. The horrible names continued into high school, and things just got worse. Gina bought into the lies that seemed like her reality. She desperately chose something that would only cause her more pain and regret. Cutting became her answer—a constant reminder of the pain inside. Caught up in the lies that deceive, Gina was lost and afraid.

The Rescue

Maybe like Gina, you feel caught up in the lies disguised as worthlessness, and you're unsure what to do. When these lies begin pulling at you, and you want out, counter that lie with God's powerful truth:

> The LORD your God is with you, he is
> mighty to save. He will take great delight

in you, he will quiet you with his love, he

will rejoice over you with singing.

(Zeph. 3:17 NIV)

I'm asking God right now to show you His heart for you on this—to write His words of love on your heart. I am asking Him to give you the courage to believe in His unconditional love for you.

LIE #4: "NO ONE WILL LOVE ME JUST FOR WHO I AM."

The Struggle

Do you ever find yourself doubting that you are truly loved and respected? Do you ever feel you need to hide the person you really are so that others will accept and love you? I know I've certainly been there!

When you believe this lie, have you noticed how willing you become to start changing even little things about yourself? It can become easy to do the things that are socially accepted and expected. So a wrong choice here and there can land you somewhere you never would have expected.

Think back to Keisha's story in chapter two. In a desperate attempt to be close to Derek and remain a part of his life, she started doing everything he did. She was so in need of love and was desperately depending on Derek to give that to her. You guessed it: She experienced tons in that relationship that she regrets. She needed assurance that she was not without hope and lasting love.

Just breathe …

You had the chance earlier to "talk" to Keisha. What would you say to her now about the hope and true love

she can find in Christ? What would you say to her if she
was having a hard time believing you and God? How
about these words for her:

> I know what I'm doing. I have it all planned
> out—plans to take care of you, not abandon
> you, plans to give you the future you hope for.
>
> *(Jer. 29:11 MSG)*

What other Scriptures might encourage Keisha?

The Rescue

God knows your heart. His words can bring comfort when you
experience serious doubts about your worth. God doesn't just love
the surface of you. His love goes deeper. He loves the whole person.
Now that's true love!

> No, despite all these things, overwhelming
> victory is ours through Christ, who loved us.
> And I am convinced that nothing can ever
> separate us from God's love. Neither death nor
> life, neither angels nor demons, neither our fears
> for today nor our worries about tomorrow—not
> even the powers of hell can separate us from
> God's love. No power in the sky above or in the
> earth below—indeed, nothing in all creation
> will ever be able to separate us from the love of
> God that is revealed in Christ Jesus our Lord.
>
> *(Rom. 8:37–39 NLT)*

I sometimes wonder why our struggles continue even when we accept God's offer of love. If you've ever felt less than beautiful, intelligent, talented, or worthy, you are not alone. I believe God knew that throughout our lives we would need His words.

I pray that you'll believe Him, accepting His words as truth. It's then that your life will be lived out differently.

LIE #5: "I'M NOT GOOD ENOUGH."

The Struggle

Ever feel you just don't have what it takes? Maybe you don't feel smart enough, talented enough, rich enough. You feel there are so many others who can do things so much greater than you can. You're just not "enough." Maybe you feel your life has no important purpose. You don't expect to be treated with any special value. Think about those words. We can so often find ourselves thinking that our lives just don't matter. God says our lives do have purpose, and He can show us what that purpose is.

Just breathe …

Take some time with God today. Tell Him exactly what you're thinking. Maybe you are struggling with knowing where you fit in this world. He wants to fill you up with hope and give you direction for an amazing future.

The Rescue

Here's what God says about this one: You were created with uniqueness. I am praying now that you would strongly believe God's opinion and His words about your life.

> Oh, don't worry; we wouldn't dare say that we
> are as wonderful as these other men who tell
> you how important they are! But they are only
> comparing themselves with each other, using
> themselves as the standard of measurement. How
> ignorant! … When people commend themselves,
> it doesn't count for much. The important
> thing is for the Lord to commend them.
>
> *(2 Cor. 10:12, 18 NLT)*

God will assure you of the great plans He has for you! Even if you can't believe those plans right now, He will help you trust.

Just breathe …

It can get pretty confusing when we are listening to everyone else's opinions of our lives. Sometimes the Ultimate Vampire can even use people in our lives to say his lies to us. Who do we really believe? Whose opinions should really matter? Why?

NEUTRALIZING THE LIES

How many times have subtle lies like the ones I just mentioned—or others I didn't mention—gone through your head?

We often go for it, buying right into the Vampire's lies. What a crazy struggle we have with our sinful nature, over and over again. And we're stubborn; I know I am. When temptations stare us in the face, we often give in. Think about the struggles that hit you right where you're most vulnerable. We may know the lies. We may have even struggled with them before—but when we're vulnerable it's easy to get drawn in.

Maybe you're not even sure when you started believing these lies. But somehow you did, and now the thoughts and habits are tough to erase. How do you sort through them to determine what is deception and what is truth? What are you supposed to do with thoughts that tear you down and cause anger, doubt, and discouragement?

Just breathe ...

Think of just one of the lies you've believed that has hurt you the most. It's pretty cool to think that God still loves us even when we're right in the middle of all the struggles. *He's for you.* Thank Him for that, and ask Him to show you how to move past the lies.

"[Mary Magdalene was] possessed by seven devils. Despite her tragic condition, she believed that she was worthy to love the Lord Jesus Christ. Somehow, she saw in His eyes the love He had for her ... she accepted His forgiveness and she loved Him with a blind passion. Mary believed the Lord's opinion of her. She took His opinion of herself rather than her own. In so doing, love was awakened within her own heart for Christ."[3]

No temptation has seized you except what is common to man. And God is faithful; he will not let you be tempted beyond what you can bear. But when you are tempted, he will also provide a way out so that you can stand up under it.

(1 Cor. 10:13 NIV)

You realize by now that the Vampire is very sneaky when targeting your life.

Sometimes it's in ways you wouldn't imagine. But God always gives you a way to escape! Let's look at some practical steps you can take—steps to make you aware of his tactics and conniving lies—that will help you choose to walk away from them.

It's really pretty simple. God is ready to give you everything you need! He speaks these words to us in 2 Peter 1:3 (NIrV):

> God's power has given us everything we need
> to lead a godly life. All of that has come to us
> because we know the One who chose us. He
> chose us because of his own glory and goodness.

1. Expose the Vampire's Lie.

Behind every temptation is an ugly lie attempting to turn you away from the truth. Ask God to reveal that lie to your heart.

Maybe you're buying into the moment and telling yourself, "This won't hurt me now and won't affect my future." That's a lie. Don't be deceived by that one.

The decisions you make now will definitely affect your future. In the moment of temptation, it's important to remember that the battle usually begins in your mind. You can't depend on willpower alone to "make the right choice" at the

✝ If allowed, the Vampire's lies can consume you. Here's what God wants you to do instead: "Fix your thoughts on what is true, and honorable, and right, and pure, and lovely, and admirable.... Then the God of peace will be with you" (Phil. 4:8–9 NLT). ✝

critical moment. That's why this next step is crucial to conquering the Vampire's lie.

2. State God's Truth.

There will be times when you're facing temptation, a lie fills your mind, and you see no way out. But you have a powerful weapon available at all times: God's truth, which brings blessings and freedom.

Whatever your hardest struggle is, God knows. And He offers you hope and courage through the promises in His Word. Just think about that—God's words alone carry that much power!

Maybe you have a hard time thinking positively about yourself. If allowed, the Vampire's lies can consume you. Here's what God wants you to do instead: "Fix your thoughts on what is true, and honorable, and right, and pure, and lovely, and admirable. Think about things that are excellent and worthy of praise. Keep putting into practice all you learned and received from me—everything you heard from me and saw me doing. Then the God of peace will be with you" (Phil. 4:8–9 NLT).

God so greatly values your life that He desires to stay right with you, always. No matter what the temptation, no matter what the lie, speak His words out loud. Say them over and over; make them your own. Write them in lipstick on your mirror, hang index cards by your light switches, cover the walls in your room with a beautiful color and paint Scripture quotes. You might start by using the verses given in this book and then move on to finding great words of God in Psalms, Ephesians, 1 John, Romans. God gives us so much to refute the lies and offer us hope!

3. Choose to Walk in His Truth.

The final, crucial step to freedom from lies is trusting, believing, and living out the promises found in God's Word. His words are greater than any other.

After reciting His words of love over and over, you can make the choice to follow Him. He'll show you how to walk it out each day. With God's help you can recognize the Vampire's deception and defuse the lies with God's truth.

Sierra had always felt very insecure, despite being popular and a cheerleader. She felt lonely and doubted there was any important purpose for her life. She talked to God about it, He talked back, and she began to listen.

God started speaking to her heart about how to revolutionize her school. See, Sierra's school was so huge that it actually had two separate cafeterias. One cafeteria was the "cool" cafeteria; the other cafeteria was known as "the ghetto." So her senior year, when by all accounts Sierra should have been hang-

I don't want you to miss out on the hope and encouragement God offers! Take a look at these promises: Psalm 103:8–13; Psalm 62:1–2, 5–8; Proverbs 3:5–6; Hebrews 12:1–3; 1 Peter 2:9; 1 John 2:5–6; 1 John 4:18–19.

ing out with her friends one last time, she started sitting in the ghetto cafeteria. Sure, it was crazy awkward at first … no one trusted the new white girl for a while. But although they called her names and ridiculed her for coming over to the "dark side," she stayed. And before long, those same girls were her friends. They spoke to her in the hallways, and she texted them on weekends.

Soon after that, sharing their struggles, she was able to pray for them and share Christ with them. Several girls have come to know the True Hero and have been baptized because of Sierra's bold step. Even more kids have seen Jesus in Sierra—she planted a seed. It changed her life … and theirs.

You see, Sierra chose to defuse the lies in her life with these words from God:

> And this is love: that we walk in obedience to
> his commands. As you have heard from the
> beginning, his command is that you walk in love.
>
> *(2 John 1:6 NIV)*

She chose to walk in love—showing Christ to others—rather than staying consumed by doubts and discouragement. What a better way to live—focusing on others and God's work rather than focusing on self.

When you choose God's truth over lies and deceptions, God frees you from confusion, doubt, anger, and depression. In place of those things, He offers safety, security, a resting place, and hope.

Isn't that what you really desire? As you get to know His amazing heart—listening to His words, knowing His love more and more throughout your life, seeing Him work in your life— you will trust His words more. You'll see how much He has for your life.

So let's go—I don't want you to miss a thing!

PRAYER OF ESCAPE

When you find yourself trapped in a lie, remember you're not out there on your own. The Holy Spirit walks with you; He will lead you through. Jesus speaks these words to you, writing them on your heart:

> I will ask the Father. And he will give you another
> Friend to help you and to be with you forever.
> The Friend is the Spirit of truth. The world
> can't accept him. That is because the world does
> not see him or know him. But you know him.
> He lives with you, and he will be in you.
> *(John 14:16–17 NIrV)*

The Enemy's lies have the potential to destroy your life like poison. They really can—moving quickly to many areas of your life and attacking your thoughts, motives, and actions. To counter that, it's essential that you seek God's life-giving serum—His Word. His powerful words really do bring life—giving hope, encouragement, healing, help, direction, and peace.

There are few people who truly take God at His word. We struggle, we doubt, we push away from the truth. Why don't we just believe what He says to us? Why don't we just trust Him? Ask yourself what it will take to step away from the lies you are believing and accept what God says to you.

Let me ask you this: Have you ever talked with God about His Word? Remember, His words are powerful. They are His promises. They are rich in life-changing potential *if you grab hold of them.*

So go to God. Take Him at His word. Here's a prayer we can pray together based on some of my favorite words of His in Isaiah 61:1–3, 9–11:

God, I want to believe Your words are truths I can trust, but so often words seem empty. I know I need to take Your every word as Truth. They can help me to change. Your words can bring hope, healing, love, and peace in a torn-up, confused me. I'm going to try. I'm going to start now.

In Your Word You say that as Your child I am loved, treasured, cherished. There is nothing that separates me from that love ... EVER! Why do I doubt You? Why do I struggle with trusting Your words as the truth I can count on?

I also must believe that Your Word goes beyond my physical ears and touches—no, it heals and restores my spirit. So now, Father, I ask You to restore my belief in me. Rejuvenate my hope in a future of blessing and peace. I struggle with my view of me. I need You to help me rely on Your words for my clear understanding. You are my Creator. You truly know me best. I must depend on Your words over any others.

You say in Your Word that what You offer me is good news, healing from brokenness, freedom for the captives, release from darkness, Your favor, comfort, provision. You even bestow beauty, gladness, praise. Those are Your truths. I accept them by faith as reality in my life. Let Your work inside me be the real deal that others can see. I need You, God. There is no one else.

CHAPTER 4

In Need of a Hero

I will be a Father to you, and you will be my
sons and daughters, says the Lord Almighty.

(2 Cor. 6:18 NIV)

In *Twilight,* Bella moves to Forks to live with her father, a man she isn't very close to. I've talked to many girls who had similar relationships with their fathers. So many girls have heartbreaking stories and unshared secrets. Sometimes there is hurt from rejection or inattentiveness, from miscommunication or judgment.

Whenever I talk about fathers with any size group of girls, the room gets very quiet. I often see tears come to their eyes. Their expressions change, they look away, they grow absolutely quiet.

I'm remembering the faces of girls who *have* shared their stories with me. I've heard their disappointments and deep hurts concerning their fathers. Many tell me about the lack of love they feel inside toward their dads. Some share that they have never met their fathers … or how they miss their dads terribly, even if they weren't great guys. We talk about the desire for closeness with a father even when we don't know him well.

I've seen sadness and tears in their eyes as they tell me how life has been with or without Dad. But, I've also seen *joy and peace* as they have come to know the true and lasting love of their Father in heaven.

So what is *your* story?

Just breathe ...

If you could describe your relationship with your dad in one word, what would it be?

Only you and God know the complete story of your life experience with your dad. For you, it might be difficult or painful to think back. If so, hold on as you read these words. I promise that God's desire is for you to know the true picture of who He really is as your loving Father.

The first thought many girls have about their dad is not always comforting, happy, or encouraging. In some cases, their bodies and their hearts have been deeply scarred. If a father figure has not respected or loved you like you deserve, you can have a hard time imagining your heavenly Father any differently. Is this *your* story?

Throughout *Twilight,* I noticed a bit of tension in Bella's relationship with her dad. You might relate to some of the things she experiences: the "one-armed hug" as she gets off the plane; the way he isn't comfortable in conversation; how often she refers to him as Charlie, not Dad; his attempt to bridge the gap between them with his gift of the red truck.

Bella remarks at one point that the best thing about her dad is that he "doesn't hover." I felt sorry, in a way, for this dad who was trying to connect with his daughter. He just didn't know how.

Throughout the story, Bella played the part of "parent" with her dad and mom. When trouble came, Bella's and her dad's roles seemed almost reversed: Bella found herself trying to save her dad's life by leading the tracker vampires away, and she outright lied to her dad to protect him. She also attempted to save her mother by running into a deadly trap.

✝ This lack of relationship with her dad culminated in Bella's lack of trust and dependence on him. ✝

This lack of relationship with her dad culminated in Bella's lack of trust and dependence on him. When she needed him the most, he was powerless to save her. Instead, she was attempting to save the ones who should have been protecting her.

Bella was in need of a hero. So are you and I.

LINDSEY'S STORY

I noticed Lindsey right away. She kept her hair in front of her face and her head down—her body language clearly indicating she didn't want to be a part of anyone's conversation. As she stepped toward me, she folded her arms across her chest. She was letting me know that she wanted to talk but didn't want to let me get too close.

I looked closely at her and saw tears welling up in her eyes. She quickly turned away, trying to keep them a secret. *Dear God,* I prayed, *help her to understand. Give me Your words. Help her to know Your love for her.* I led her to a quiet seat, and she told me her story.

Lindsey's biological father left when she was two. Her mother told her many times that before he left, he said, "You can have the kid." He didn't even go to the trouble of calling her by name.

As she grew up, Lindsey's mother often reminded her how hard it was to feed and clothe her and find a place for them to live. It didn't take long for Lindsey to feel unwanted and unworthy of love.

Things got worse when Lindsey's mother moved them in with the man who would become her stepdad. He told Lindsey she was fat, stupid, and a waste of space. And when her mother left the house, he would force himself on Lindsey.

This hopeless situation lasted for nearly two years. Lindsey wanted to ask God for help, but she didn't think He'd listen. And she never once believed He cared.

Finally, protective services intervened, and Lindsey was placed in a series of foster homes. In the year prior to attending my conference, she had been living with a family who loved God and made it obvious to Lindsey that they loved her as well. She watched the father of this family with his children and felt her heart break every time he wrapped his arms around his daughters. He spent time with them. He showed them he really cared, even about little things.

"That's what I want," Lindsey said, wiping her tears away with the palm of her hand. "I want to feel safe. But I don't feel like I deserve it. And I don't know how to accept it."

I grabbed Lindsey's hand and shared with her, "God's love isn't an impersonal love that disappoints us." I told her that His love was unconditional and unchanging. We talked and prayed, asking God to show her this unending love.

She listened but was skeptical. She had been hurt and disappointed too many times to believe someone's words ... even God's. I knew God understood. He knows better than anyone the difficult memories that keep playing over and over in her mind.

SEARCHING FOR DADDY'S LOVE

Because of the years and years of hurt and disappointment in Lindsey's life, she didn't know how to accept the true love of the Father. I know it's tough—without experiencing a father's love from our earthly dad, we have a hard time accepting the enormous love God has for us.

What is it that we are all truly searching for? We want to be respected, intensely loved—to have someone who is forever loyal, unselfishly true to our heart. That is the heart of a hero we are longing for. A true hero is one who would lay down his own life for you out of the truest, purest love and devotion imaginable.

Some girls don't picture a father as the hero they would need or desire. Maybe it's because they don't understand what a hero truly is, or the relationship they have experienced has been a difficult one. It is that little girl's heart inside that grows up believing Daddy is supposed to be the hero in her life. Often, this is not the case.

Don't you know that the Ultimate Vampire must take great delight in these struggles we face? Imagine his delight as he views so many hurting girls with misconceptions of what a father really should be in their lives. He must hope (as the Enemy of our soul) to distract our attention from the eternal Father, who provides rescue from heartbreak, emptiness, or fear.

YOUR DAD CONNECTION

Just breathe …

So if you and I were to sit down together and talk right now, what would you tell me about your dad? How would you describe him? Would you try to change the subject?

Maybe you'd tell me that your relationship is close—that he is there for you, that he loves you deeply. If this is true of your relationship with your dad, you have a rare gift. Maybe you'd tell me you've never really known him. Maybe you feel rejected by him. Maybe there's a girlfriend in his life, and you don't know where you and your family fit in anymore. Maybe you're not even sure where he is.

You might feel like your dad's love is based on what you achieve in school or whether you excel in sports. Maybe you struggle with feeling like you're never good enough. I've talked with many girls who have felt this way.

Gem of Truth

"A father to the fatherless, a defender of widows, is God in his holy dwelling. God sets the lonely in families" (Ps. 68:5–6 NIV). God really cares about those who need a dad in their lives!

I do know this: We each long for that father-daughter connection. It's how God has made us. And sometimes, lacking that connection, we attempt to fill it with other relationships. It's nice to receive attention, sweet gifts, and text messages from a guy you're really into. But I've also seen life "shut down" for girls who depend so much on that guy for happiness. Remember how devastated Bella was during Edward's long absence in *New Moon?* Did you see how such total dependence

Stories of Dads

Secrets. "He's hurt me in ways I've told no one.... I don't like to think about him."

Misunderstanding. "He doesn't get me. He wants me to talk to him … but I have nothing to say."

Noncommunicative. "I must not be very important to him because he has nothing to say to me. I would never tell him anything really important to me. He doesn't care."

Too busy for me. "Oh, he's home … but not really. I see him, but I don't really think he sees me."

Surface love. "He tries to basically buy my heart—and you can't do that. He shows up handing me a credit card and expects a hug, thinking everything will be fine … and it's not."

Hypocrite. "He acts totally different when he's at church or around his friends from work. The person he is at home is not the same person they know. I don't trust him."

on one person could be harmful to her? How she lost interest in her friends, her school, and any other part of her life?

I've witnessed the struggles girls face with guys and the emptiness they continue to feel inside. And I think this emptiness can often be tracked to a disconnect with their dad. This kind of hole can leave a daughter's heart vulnerable, insecure, and lacking in self-worth.

EMPTY REPLACEMENT

It's these "dad struggles" that often lead girls to easily accept the Vampire's entice-ments as a substitute. They fall into unhealthy relationships and struggle with choices that bring painful consequences.

Does the story always play out this way? Absolutely not. But too often it does.

I remember my conversation with a girl named Jackie. She explained how painful it was to feel that her dad always tried to prove his love with his credit card. She admitted an obsession with a "need to buy … all the time." But money couldn't buy the love she craved inside. Additionally, Jackie always felt she needed a boyfriend. But maybe it was the emptiness she was feeling inside that hurt most of all. Boyfriends were her way to cover up the hurt, an attempt to fill the gap inside.

Dedra always felt like she struggled with her weight. She constantly worked out at the gym and watched every morsel of food she put in her mouth. When she was diagnosed as anorexic, suddenly everyone was super tuned in to her. Her every move was analyzed. Her dad brought up constantly how much worry and concern she was placing on her family and told her she'd better "straighten up." Dedra had believed that her dad never accepted her size—and now he didn't seem to care about understanding her struggle either.

These are sadly very common stories today: A daughter's heart is crushed; she feels misunderstood and alone. If a father figure has not respected or loved her as she deserves, she can have a hard time imagining her heavenly Father being any different.

THE DADDY GAP

I believe there's a longing in our hearts that desires that close connection with our Father. It's a God-sized spot inside. We have a longing in our hearts for a true, meaningful, *perfect* daddy relationship.

I promise you this: He is *for you!*

God created this spot because He wants to fill our hearts with His amazing love. God talks about that in Galatians 4:6–7: "And because we are his children, God has sent the Spirit of his Son into our hearts, prompting us to call out, 'Abba, Father.' Now you are no longer a slave but God's own child. And since you are his child, God has made you his heir" (NLT).

As a part of God's family, as His child, you are given every privilege of being His. You can run to Him with anything on your mind. He calls you His daughter, and you carry His name. There is *honor* that comes with that—just think about who He is. He is proud to be called your Dad!

His is the only undying love that can truly satisfy our hearts. But for some reason, that fact is still hard to accept. Each of us wants a perfect dad here on earth. No matter how long we search or how much we dream, we won't find him.

It must be sad for the Lord—who has such unconditional love for His kids—to see His love pushed away or ignored because of an incorrect understanding of who He really is. God says in 1 John 3:16 that His love is deep and true. He laid down His life for us … for you. That's the kind of Father He is.

ARMS AROUND THE TRUTH

It may be really tough to put your arms around this one. But think about this: There is no one in this world who can give you the absolute love that you need.

As His child, think about the father you have in God—your heavenly Father. In reality, the relationship between you and God is the perfect dad-daughter relationship you've been searching for. There it is. Hard to imagine it could be that simple. But the fact is, God offers you the most amazing love that trumps any other love you would receive in a lifetime.

Whatever your story, you can know that God has this amazing Daddy's love *for you*. It's a true statement: Your Father in heaven has everlasting love for you—a love without end! Listen to what He says

to you in 2 Corinthians 6:18: "I will be a Father to you, and you will
be my sons and daughters, says the Lord Almighty" (NIV).

Regardless of how close or how distant your relationship is with
your dad on this earth, know that God cherishes you. Pretty amazing
to realize, isn't it?

And He demonstrated His love by offering the most amazing
gift of His Son, Jesus. The ultimate sacrifice was made, and we received Jesus as our true Immortal Hero, who gave His life for us! That's the kind of love our Father offers.

✝ Listen to what He says to you in 2 Corinthians 6:18: "I will be a Father to you, and you will be my sons and daughters, says the Lord Almighty" (NIV). ✝

He's never leaving, and He's offering you His time, complete
acceptance, and unconditional love. What more could you want
from a father? Let Him show you how faithful He really is.

STRONG CONFIDENCE

Taking a trip to the park with my dad, I clambered up onto a huge
stone ledge. I had climbed slightly out of his reach, and Dad called
for me to jump to him.

There I was, a very girlie four-year-old blonde with ponytails
and ribbons, calling out to my dad to *pleeeeeeease* come closer. All
I could see was what looked like a huge gap between my dad and
me. I wanted a lot more reassurance before attempting that jump.

Of course, Dad knew he would catch me. But my little-girl heart
was afraid, and my mind was focused on the fear.

Maybe you know about God's love but are still afraid. Are you
doubting, maybe pulling away, or even questioning His love for you?

Are you afraid to make that jump? One very cool thing about His love is that He offers it but never insists that you accept it. He wants the acceptance to be *your choice.*

I love God's words in Hebrews 13:5: "Never will I leave you; never will I forsake you" (NIV). He will never turn us away.

And did you know He is extra close to those without dads? I love to hear that. Psalm 10:14 tells us that God is the "helper of the fatherless" (NIV). If you've never really had a dad, I pray that verse can be of particular comfort to you.

In Zephaniah 3:17 it says, "He will quiet you with his love, he will rejoice over you with singing" (NIV).

Just breathe ...

Don't you just love that? Look back and read those words (Zeph. 3:17) again and let them sink in. Take a breath and ask God to quiet you with His love.

When you are really upset, torn apart by the words or actions of your dad or someone else here on this earth, God hears you and is present with you. His arms surround you and comfort you.

As little boys, both of my sons cried out many nights for comfort and love. They wanted to be held close and reassured—and I loved to do that for them. In the same way, our Father God hears you and wants to comfort you when you are crying out. He is ready to hold you close—to quiet you with His love.

In his book *The Father Heart of God,* Floyd McClung wrote, "God heard you speak your first real word. He watched with delight as you spent hours alone exploring new textures with baby hands. He treasures the memories of your childhood laughter. There has never been another child like you, and there never will be."[1]

You can hear those words … but are they hard for you to believe?

Lindsey never had a father who delighted in her. She was never told how beautiful she was or how proud she made her dad. She never heard her father cheer as she took her first steps or learned to ride a bike. But her heavenly Father was cheering and delighting in His little girl. The trouble was, Lindsey didn't know it.

HE'LL MEET YOU THERE

Deep inside, we all want someone who is present—someone who's really there. We want to trust our dad when he says he loves us. We want to know that he loves spending time with us. We don't want to feel pressured to be perfect or to be anyone different. We basically want an unconditional love that our earthly dads can never provide.

While reading *Twilight,* I often wondered how differently Bella might have acted if she had a dad she could confide in. A dad who understood her heart and had her trust.

Look what God promises us. God speaks about His love in Isaiah 49:16: "See, I have engraved you on the palms of my hands" (NIV).

Author Claire Cloninger wrote, "In some mysterious way our names were carved into the palms of God's hands by the nails of the cross. I believe those nails so painfully driven into the flesh of His Only Begotten that awful day on Calvary have written us into His life in such a way that He can never, never forget us…. He is our Father, and we are His children."[2]

Imagine: your name written permanently by the hand of God. What a cool picture! God did not create you to forget about you. His love is always available for you. That's the kind of dad He is.

So when you're questioning whether God could really have this kind of love and care for you, know that He meets you there. Even in the midst of all the

doubts inside. As His child, you can set your heart at rest in His presence, even when your heart tells you something different. You can relax and know "He's got you," even when you're scared inside. God says:

> This then is how we know that we belong to the
> truth, and how we set our hearts at rest in his
> presence whenever our hearts condemn us. For God
> is greater than our hearts, and he knows everything.
>
> *(1 John 3:19–20 NIV)*

He is greater than our hearts—don't you love that? He knows the hurts you have inside, and He knows what you need. Sometimes we don't even know what needs we have, but God sees and will meet them. You're that important to Him.

KATY'S STORY

It was near the end of a conference when a teen said, "Thank you for what you told us about God being our dad. It's been hard to describe the hurt I've been feeling really deep inside."

I knew I was hearing just the tip of what had been bottled up inside her for a long time. After her parents' divorce, Katy saw her dad only occasionally. She would try calling him, but many times she felt like her dad was in a hurry to get off the phone or like she was bothering him. His plans to see her would often fall through, and she would feel abandoned by him once again. This happened over and over again.

He continually gave excuses, and this left Katy frustrated and angry. She couldn't understand why she felt like the parent so many times. What about the little girl inside of her that needed her daddy? She felt crushed and very alone.

You might know how badly it hurts to feel rejected or dishonored by your dad or by someone else in authority in your life. It can be very tough—I've heard so many stories of girls who have desperately searched for this love in others and have been crushed at the end.

I could see how very overwhelmed Katy was to discover how personal and dependable God's love was for her. *He* was dependable. She could trust what *He had to say.* She could trust His love!

She began to understand that her heavenly Father had been there for her. She had been held by Him. She found it so amazing that He had been with her all those times when she thought she was

Heart of the Father

Do you know how important you are to Him?

∼ God stays right with you—you are that important (Ps. 23).

∼ God chooses you—you are His (Eph. 1:11–14).

∼ God guarded your life even before you were born—you are His treasure (Ps. 139:13–18).

∼ God's love will never leave—He commits to stand by you no matter what (Rom. 8:38–39).

Thanks, Dad

I am blessed beyond measure to be loved and cherished by my amazing dad! I thank God for his strength of character, faithfully loving heart, and commitment to me and my family. I pray you have known a father on this earth that has reflected in some way your heavenly Father. If you have, thank him today!

standing all alone. Those gaps inside her heart could finally be filled with a love that would never leave.

God's healing began in the deepest part of Katy's life. She is learning to trust His heart and is coming to know Him even more intimately as her Abba Daddy. Abba is one of God's favorite names for Himself. The word *Abba* expresses an especially close relationship that God has with His kids. If someone in the Bible would have said, "Abba, I need you," it would have been translated as, "Daddy, I need you." So when we call out to Him, "Daddy, I need you," He hears us!

Isn't that awesome? We have the privilege of calling out to God, our Abba, at any time and trusting Him with whatever is on our minds or hearts. It's a pretty amazing deal. Katy came to know and trust the love of her Abba Daddy, and I pray that you will too.

TEXTING GOD

Okay, so if you could text God a message (which is basically what you do when you pray), what would you like to tell Him, daughter to Dad?

Maybe you're not sure what to say. If that's the case, start by reading some of God's thoughts of you. Check out this verse in Zephaniah 3:17 (NLT):

> For the LORD your God is living among you. He is
> a mighty savior. He will take delight in you with

What Is a Dad?

"A dad is someone who wants to catch you before you fall but instead picks you up, brushes you off, and lets you try again. A dad is someone who wants to keep you from making mistakes but instead lets you find your own way, even though his heart breaks in silence when you get hurt. A dad is someone who holds you when you cry, scolds you when you break the rules, shines with pride when you succeed, and has faith in you even when you fail."—Susan Ceylise

"They say that from the instant he lays eyes on her, a father adores his daughter. Whoever she grows up to be, she is always to him that little girl in pigtails. She makes him feel like Christmas. In exchange, he makes a secret promise not to see the awkwardness of her teenage years, the mistakes she makes or the secrets she keeps."—Unknown

gladness. With his love, he will calm all your fears. He will rejoice over you with joyful songs.

These are some of my favorite comforting words from our heavenly Father. What hope! He is with you. He is your strength and is very capable of taking care of you.

He is tuned in to the details of your life. You can talk with Him … no catching up needed. He's been with you through it all. So think of the things you've always wanted to say to your dad and just never could. What have you wished he knew about you? You can say these things to God.

Just breathe …

Take some time right now and just talk to your amazing Father in heaven. He's listening.

PART II

Soul Redeemed

Teach me to do your will, for you are my
God. May your gracious Spirit lead me
forward on a firm footing. For the glory of
your name, O LORD, preserve my life.

(Ps. 143:10–11 NLT)

CHAPTER 5

Desperate for Forgiveness

To him who loves us and has freed us
from our sins by shedding his blood.

(Rev. 1:5 NLT)

When I got my first look at the cover design for this book, I immediately saw cool, clean, and simple ... and a flower that was *perfectly
white*. I wasn't sure about the flower. "Perfect" totally contradicts
how many girls see themselves. It contradicts how I see myself. We
will never achieve "perfect" in this lifetime. "Perfect" is what I will
never be. But as I looked and thought, I realized this image *was* just
right—because of His Son. *This is how God sees me.*

I began to think about how desperate we are for His forgiveness.
But what really amazes me is Christ's unbelievable acceptance of us
despite our imperfect selves. No one else could offer us anything
close to that.

Maybe women all throughout history have thought about this
same concept. Maybe the chase for beauty and perfection has driven
us back to questions of why we would desire them to begin with. It's

when we come to the end of our search that we realize who it is that accepts us, loves us, and forgives us right where we are.

A COMMON HARLOT

Rahab moved to answer the knock at the door, her tunic floating behind her like a heavily perfumed reminder of the life she lived. She expected to find the same guarded, shamefaced expression she saw on the faces of her regular guests. Speaking respectfully in quiet voices, the two men bowed low as they entered her home. Rahab's eyes opened wide in surprise. These men, she quickly realized, seemed very different.

Their chivalry intrigued her. Never had she received such treatment from men. Did they know who she was? She must learn more of these men and the motive behind their visit.

Prostitution was the only life she knew, and every day she lived covered in guilt and shame. Little did she imagine there could be incredible plans for her future. But *God* knew. From the beginning, He knew her awesome story of rescue and redemption.

The amazing story began when these two Hebrew men, spies sent by Joshua to check out the city, came to Rahab's doorstep that night. The Israelite army needed information in order to prepare for an attack on Jericho. Rahab needed those spies to come find her and share the good news of the Lord God and His plan for her life.

> "The definition of redemption specifies that the only redeemer is Jesus.... [He] is the only one that has the perfect ransom and perfect gift to save us."—Access-Jesus.com[1]

God led the spies to her house for the purpose of saving Rahab and her family. In turn, God allowed her to play a vital role in leading the nation of Israel to victory.

Bottom line: God chose this woman to fulfill His plan. Rahab—the outcast, the prostitute—was rescued and given a divine mission by God Himself.

Did her sin keep her from being used by God? Absolutely not. God chose to use her in the midst of it. He took someone bearing shame and regret, someone who must have felt unworthy, and saved her—placing her in a position of honor among the greatest in the history of Israel! Through this God-encounter, Rahab became a respectable woman.

Rahab's Honor

~ Rahab is listed among the famous heroes of faith along with Moses, Abraham, and Noah (Hebrews 11:31).

~ She is described as righteous. I like to think of the word *righteous* as a description of someone who is *choosing to make right choices* (James 2:25).

~ Married Salmon and her son was Boaz, a godly, prominent leader who married Ruth (Ruth 4:21).

~ Rahab was the many-times-over great-grandmother of Jesus the Messiah, who came to the world to bring sinners, including harlots, into the kingdom of God (Matthew 1:5).

SARAH'S STORY

Often I think the Lord brings me to each conference event for one girl. This time it was for Sarah. Ours was a conversation that drew me into every word. Here in front of me was not just an interested *Twilight* fan but one who could quote every line. Sarah knew the characters' every move from the books and the movie. She talked about the scenes as if she had experienced them herself.

The *Twilight* connection was how we started talking. I wanted to know what it was that drew her into the movie. She wanted to talk about it. So we did. What I learned through hanging out with Sarah was her deep desire to be accepted and her longing to be truly loved. She had connected with the story of Edward and Bella because they were experiencing so much of what she thought she needed inside. *She* wanted connection, acceptance, love … and a hero. She had questions and wanted answers.

It wasn't the first time Sarah had heard about how Christ had chosen her and extended His gift of complete forgiveness and love. But she said this time something was different. I saw on her face the incredible change going on inside. The Immortal Hero was offering His love and commitment to her. No matter what her difficult experiences and regretful choices, He loved and forgave her. This was the greatest offer of love she would ever find!

After Sarah left the conference, we stayed in touch. A few weeks later, in an email, she shared that she felt her life crumbling. Once again, the guys, the choices, and the life she lived before she came to the conference were staring at her, begging her to return to them. And she did. Not long after that, her feelings of unworthiness and shame returned too.

You may have felt that way before.

THE VICIOUS CYCLE

You may, like Rahab or my friend Sarah, feel stuck in a trap. Life goes on day after day, because what else can you do? Every day you live with the memory of some horrible experience or choice—a relationship that turned to regret, a sin you cannot seem to move past.

When you feel lost and without any purpose, it's difficult to find hope for the future, to move beyond the sin. But think about this: By accepting God's forgiveness and going forward, you may one day be blessed with an opportunity to be used mightily by God, as Rahab was.

Remember, the Ultimate Vampire delights in flaunting your emptiness before your face. It's like when you look in the mirror and see only flaws. God looks in that same mirror and sees a beautiful you that He designed uniquely with value and purpose. Looking at yourself through His eyes is a perspective of forgiveness, and it's such an important step in breaking free from a lifestyle of emptiness.

There was a scene in *Twilight* where, late one night, Bella climbed into her truck with tears streaming down her face. After a dangerous encounter with a menacing vampire, Bella's life was threatened, and she was caught in a dangerous chase. She wanted safety, but her father wasn't aware of the dangers. Her mother was too far away. Could Edward really protect her? Not really. He admitted he put her in harm's way to begin with.

She was afraid. She desperately needed to be rescued. She needed to feel safe.

Like Bella, sometimes we don't want to admit our desperate need for a rescue. Will we look weak? Incapable? Unable to deal with life? Inside we may question our strength and abilities. We know what we need but are afraid to ask. Our Savior alone offers rescue—with no strings attached.

The ultimate rescue story:

> And this hope will not lead to disappointment.
> For we know how dearly God loves us,
> because he has given us the Holy Spirit
> to fill our hearts with his love.
> When we were utterly helpless, Christ came at

just the right time and died for us sinners. Now,
most people would not be willing to die for an
upright person, though someone might perhaps be
willing to die for a person who is especially good.
But God showed his great love for us by sending
Christ to die for us while we were still sinners.

(Rom. 5:5–8 NLT)

God promises to be with you throughout the story of your life.

✝ **Where you see a hopeless future filled with hurt and longing, He sees the opportunity for a new beginning!** ✝

Where you see failure, He sees hope and promise. Where you see broken dreams and crushed promises, He sees potential for greatness. Where you see a hopeless future filled with hurt and longing, He sees the opportunity for a new beginning! He offers to move you *toward* that very hope.

WHEN LOVE SPEAKS

I've often seen hope best conveyed through love's action. It can be these actions that prove forgiveness and undying love beyond our own.

Hitting the streets of Chicago late one night, a group of college students were given a unique outreach assignment: to demonstrate Christ's love to prostitutes on the street corners of the city. Presenting each woman with a beautiful rose, the students spoke Christ's undying love into their lives. Whew … pretty amazing idea!

After one unforgettable night of ministry, the students gathered to share their stories. They talked about one woman who stared in disbelief and immediately began to weep. She had never experienced a gesture like this with nothing expected in return. I wonder what questions were going through her mind. I wonder if she, like Rahab,

> Hope is the flower that blooms from the seed of faith.

was touched deeply by God's Spirit at that moment. I have to believe she was.

That night, those women were given a taste of Christ's unconditional forgiveness. It must have spoken volumes to their hearts. God's truth is capable of trumping every lie and deception you believe. God's unconditional acceptance points toward the hope of forgiveness.

THE "YUCK" LIST

Hundreds of times now, I've spoken to girls about God's forgiveness and shared His unchanging acceptance and unconditional love for them. I have seen their desire to believe His promises written all over their faces. They're ready for a new start. We take action.

They're each given a sheet of paper and a pen; then, toward the end of the session, I give them some time to write out all the "yuck"—the stuff inside they can't seem to get past.

Something happens during those moments that's hard to explain. It's a *relief* for many girls to finally pour out their heart without fear of being rejected or judged for what they say. Many have said it's like a huge weight is being lifted. I think they finally *get it*—God is there ready to listen and ready to help them through whatever it is that they may be struggling with inside.

There are times when I've seen their sheets so filled with notes to God that there wasn't any room left on the paper! I know their honesty touches His heart.

We then take this list to God in prayer, asking for His forgiveness and healing or whatever is needed. Finally, we rip those sheets up into hundreds of little pieces! It's a symbolic moment. What a release … what a relief!

Getting it down on paper isn't always a fun thing, but it's a beginning. To literally leave all our "yuck" with the Lord, who then takes it and removes it from our lives—that's an amazing moment. I have seen tears, hugs, and many prayers from girls. There's a real peace and celebration in that moment.

> "O Lord, you are so good, so ready to forgive, so full of unfailing love for all who ask for your help."
> —Psalm 86:5 (NLT)

What's the "yuck" inside *you* that you really wish you could move past? Maybe it's a crazy relationship with memories you wish you could delete. Maybe you've been hurt very deeply by a friend and you need healing inside. Are there habits in your life you're not happy with? Are there things you just don't like about yourself?

Whatever your "yuck," God wants to begin the process of healing and change you on the inside. Maybe some wrong choices you've made are coming to mind right now. It doesn't matter how little or how huge they are; you can talk to God about each one.

I've included something special for you in this book: a page to write out all of these things. Just spend time talking to the Lord and ask Him to reveal what's in your heart that you desperately need Him to take. The first step to receiving forgiveness and a new beginning is being honest with what's going on inside your life. He wants to help you move forward!

After you've written out your list of "yuck" and talked through it with God, I want you to tear this page into tiny pieces and throw those pieces away. So go ahead. Rip it out. It's time for a new beginning.

THE FORGIVENESS MOMENT

Tearing out your "yuck" page symbolizes the fact that He takes your sins and removes them entirely. Can you imagine that? From God's perspective, they are gone forever; it's as if they never existed.

Let's check out these words from God's heart:

> For as high as the heavens are above the earth,
> so great is his love for those who fear him;
> as far as the east is from the west, so far has
> he removed our transgressions from us.
>
> *(Ps. 103:11–12 NIV)*

God wants us to recognize the "yuck" inside so something can be done about it. He understands why you've made the choices you have. Keep talking to Him about it, then ask Him to show you what to do next.

Christ actually forgives everything that we bring to Him. Seems unbelievable, doesn't it? Then He fully reassures us of His love and of new beginnings. He speaks His words of hope.

IT ALL GOES BACK

Let's take a look at Genesis 3:8. "Then the man and his wife heard the sound of the LORD God as he was walking in the garden in the cool of the day, and they hid from the LORD God among the trees of the garden" (NIV). Adam and Eve were hiding; they were ashamed. They must have felt afraid, unworthy, and guilty.

There's a theme in this chapter. As with Rahab, Adam and Eve, and you and me today, humans struggle with feeling *disqualified* from receiving God's love. But Christ's forgiveness is so much bigger than that.

Let's look at what happened next to Adam and Eve, in verse 9: "But the LORD God called to the man, 'Where are you?'" (NIV).

God had not pulled His love away. He responded to them. He sought them out in love. He came to rescue them. I love that! It shows that God came looking for them when He could have just destroyed everything and started over.

This is quite different from the Ultimate Vampire's plan to cause destruction in our lives and then abandon us entirely, isn't it? Think about the contrast that God offers. Right in the middle of paradise, His kids blew it. He knew exactly what was going on. God found His creation in the middle of their sin and still loved them despite their shame. He loved them right through those times, right after they had both chosen to go against God's words to them. He *continued* to seek after them with His love.

God wants you to hear His words of comfort and encouragement!

~ I will always be with you (Ps. 139:7–10)!

~ I'll keep believing in you no matter what (Ps. 103:8–13)!

~ Your future can still be filled with hope (Jer. 29:11)!

~ I will always be strong for you (Ps. 71:3).

~ You can rely on my love (1 John 4:16).

~ You can give me all your worries, because I care for you (1 Peter 5:7).

Think about what took place in the garden. Adam and Eve committed the first sin … the first act of disobedience … the first show of disloyalty. This must have broken God's heart. His precious creation chose to disobey Him—to reject the words of their loving Father.

Despite their choices, God sought after Adam and Eve with His unconditional love—it's the most amazing part of the whole forgiveness moment. And He did the same for Rahab. In the midst of a sinful life, she was chosen and used mightily by God. The same is true for you and for me. God confronts our sins, and we experience the consequences of our actions. He deals with the sin—our wrong choices—yet He continues to love us still. That's a picture of His love and grace that's just unexplainable.

Isn't it great that God also fully reaches out to us and continues to seek after us each day, even in the middle of our "yuck"? Imagine perfect hands taking your stuff—the "yuck" stuff that you don't even like to think about. That's His amazing love. Even when we have greatly disappointed Him, He *still* chooses to be our rescuer.

A DESPERATE PRAYER

Even in the midst of that beautiful picture of forgiveness, sometimes doubts may surface.

Remember my friend Sarah from the beginning of the chapter? She experienced those doubts and then deeply questioned God's forgiveness yet again. But God was there for her, and another email came to me months later telling me that she had found hope and healing in His faithfulness to her. *He is faithful* even when we have chosen not to be.

Sometimes it may be difficult to forgive *ourselves*. I know because it has happened to me. Are there things you're thinking about now that seem to constantly resurface? Are you ready to leave them behind you? God wants this for your life. No matter what it is, He is greater. He knows your heart already.

Maybe your prayer to Him could be something like this:

> *Lord Jesus, You know the details of my life better than anyone. I'm so sorry. Please forgive me for _____. Thank You for Your amazing forgiveness and love! Lord, please show me how it's possible to put this behind me. Give me courage to forgive myself.*
>
> *Jesus, into Your hands, I give _____ to You. I will not choose to hold on to it or look back any longer. I thank You, Lord, for Your love and for offering me new hope.*
>
> *I give You all of my doubts and the fears I have inside. I know that through the forgiveness only You could offer me, I do have a new beginning. Right now I choose to forgive myself. Thank You, Lord!*
>
> *Now I ask You to show me how to accept Your complete forgiveness and move forward differently. Help me to honor You with my life. Thank You again, Jesus! In Your precious name, Amen.*

What a step you've taken! Even as I write these words to you, God is bringing things to mind about my life that need to be different. I'm also going to talk with Him right now. What an awesome Savior we have! He provides an escape (Rom. 8:1–2).

CHAPTER 6

Rescued by Love

Who can be compared with the LORD
our God, who is enthroned on high?
He stoops to look down on heaven and
on earth. He lifts the poor from the
dust and the needy from the garbage
dump. He sets them among princes.

(Ps. 113:5–8 NLT)

❧

As Thomas approached the Dumpster behind his flower shop, he heard a strange sound. *The moment I open the Dumpster, that stray cat is going to jump right out,* he thought. But as he drew closer, Thomas knew this sound wasn't coming from a cat.

The cry grew louder. Thomas knew he needed to find the source of this cry, and fast. He pulled open the lid, climbed into the dirty, smelly Dumpster, and began pulling out bag after bag. "Keep crying so I can find you!" he shouted, grabbing a large plastic bag that had been knotted tightly shut. Something in the bag was moving. Thomas's hands trembled as he ripped it open.

Inside he found a newborn baby. She couldn't be more than a few hours old.

Later, doctors would estimate her time of birth at four in the after-noon; Thomas discovered her less than two hours later. The "miracle baby" survived with a mere hairline fracture to her skull.

Rescue

to free from confinement, danger, or evil; save, deliver
—Merriam-Webster OnLine

It's unbelievable, isn't it? A beautiful baby girl rescued from a Dumpster miraculously survives and, weeks later, is placed with a wonderful Christian family. Sounds like a "happily ever after."

But if you stop to think about it, she was literally *thrown away* at birth. You can understand why, years later, Rachael found it difficult to believe she could be a dream in God's heart.

Just breathe …

My mom is one incredible, godly woman. I wish you could meet her. God's compassion and love pours richly from her life! She has this amazing gift of making others feel incredibly special. She's given me the picture of God's devoted love right here on this earth. Take a minute to thank God for someone in your life who has shown you God's love.

THE DREAM OF YOU

I remember the day I met Rachael after one of my conferences. Her long dark hair, sparkling brown eyes, and sweet laugh did not even hint at the kind of story she was about to share.

Despite her amazing rescue from the Dumpster, Rachael was still fighting a deep battle fifteen years later. God had placed her in a loving Christian family, but she was hurting inside. She questioned the details over and over again. I could hear the hurt in her words and see it in her tears. Her struggle was with feelings of rejection.

Don't you know the Ultimate Vampire so delights in that struggle? He loves it when you are discouraged, haunted, or depressed. He catches you in moments of weakness and *rejoices* in that. To him it's a victory. Unbelievable, isn't it?

I saw up close how the Vampire was using Rachael's miraculous story to discourage her. I sat on the stage with her as she talked with me about this very

> "Hope is the expectation that something outside of ourselves, something or someone external, is going to come to our rescue and we will live happily ever after."—Dr. Robert Anthony

painful part of her past. Tears streaming down her face, she asked, "Why does this have to be my story? It's really not fair that there is nothing I can do to change it. I was a *baby*. Why did my parents want to throw me away?"

There was no way to go back and erase that part of Rachael's life. But I could share these comforting words from God with her: "I will not fail you or abandon you" (Josh. 1:5 NLT). That promise includes Rachael. God says to her and to you, "When your father and mother forsake you, I will be with you."

I could tell Rachael with honesty that *God had been with her.* He sat in the middle of all that muck in the Dumpster and watched over His sweet girl. He cradled her…. He held her close.

Rachael's heavenly Father stayed even when her biological father and mother rejected her. She needed to know that. He never left Rachael—not from the moment she was conceived. God rescued Rachael and continues to be with her throughout every moment of her life.

THE FIGHT FOR YOUR LIFE

Rachael is not alone in her feelings or her battle, and neither are you. God wants to comfort you just as He comforted her. In the middle of all that you may be dealing with, He wants to rescue

you as He rescued her. Isn't that amazing? The God of the universe never, ever gives up on you. You are cherished and hoped for; you are a treasured dream of His heart.

Maybe you struggle with believing this could be true. If so, you're not alone. And one of the biggest stumbling blocks

> "I waited patiently for the LORD to help me, and he turned to me and heard my cry. He lifted me out of the pit of despair, out of the mud and the mire. He set my feet on solid ground and steadied me as I walked along."
> — Psalm 40:1–2 (NLT)

of trusting His love is not knowing how to receive love from others or love from God.

We can find ourselves manipulated by one of Satan's most effective lies: *You are not worthy of God's attention or love. You are not worthy of a rescue.* The Enemy wants you to feel unaccepted and unlovable.

It's a lie that easily captures your mind and heart. Think about it. You are surrounded by all the love you could ever need in Him, and yet you don't see it. It's one of the Vampire's most successful illusions. He wants you blinded to the safety, acceptance, and unconditional love that can be found only in your heavenly Father's arms.

He's deceiving, isn't he? If you're blinded to God's love, you will seek acceptance and love somewhere else.

In the *Twilight* film and books, Bella longs in the same way for love, acceptance, and safety. She has a detached relationship with both her dad and her mom; she has resigned herself to living in a place she detests; she is anxious about making new friends; and she's feeling lonely.

On top of all that, Bella finds herself drawn to a gorgeous, mysterious guy. She can't stop thinking about him, despite the unsettling knowledge that something is very wrong. This much-quoted paragraph from the book summarizes her feelings:

> *About three things I was absolutely positive.*
> *First, Edward was a vampire. Second, there*
> *was part of him—and I didn't know how*
> *potent that part might be—that thirsted for*
> *my blood. And third, I was unconditionally*
> *and irrevocably in love with him.*

Just breathe ...

If you could, like Bella, begin to write your story, what three things would you be absolutely positive about in your life?

1.

2.

3.

Edward represents mystery, intrigue, and a dangerous kind of adventure—and Bella's heart is swept away with the excitement of being chosen by this handsome loner.

Eventually, what Bella wants—what becomes most important to her—outweighs rational logic. The movie's closing line signifies that her fate is already sealed: "I know what I want."

FINDING TRUE LOVE

Girls have shared with me that they want the "real deal" in their relationships. They want to believe that someone would risk *everything* for them in the name of love. I think that's what we find so compelling about the Bella-Edward story. Without considering the consequences, we see it as the reckless, consuming love we're looking for—the kind of love, in fact, that we would die for.

Recently, I asked a group of girls to share their take on Edward. Several eagerly responded that Edward is "the guy I wish was for real." He's a great-looking, attentive protector, and he's so into Bella. They are caught up in what they call his "sacrificial love" because he constantly resists his lust for her blood.

I can understand why girls see Edward as somewhat noble. But is *this* a true picture of sacrifice? Or is it the illusion of a hero?

Now I want to ask you another question. What if there really is someone so perfect, and He is in love with you?

In fact, there is—so much so that there's no comparison. Listen to the words of the True Hero: "Greater love has no one than this, that he lay down his life for his friends" (John 15:13 NIV). Right there is the heart of your Ultimate Rescuer.

God created you with a desire to be pursued with a pure and

passionate love. When Jesus submitted to death on a cross—the worst
kind of death, according to Philippians 2:8—He literally laid down His
life for you. In other words, His life was sacrificed in exchange for yours.

God boldly says that He stands with you and pursues you as *your
Rescuer*. He is your literal Savior—your Ultimate Hero. God's love
for you is the purest rescue story because it does not contain a hint
of selfishness.

And we need a rescue. We're sinners, and without Him—even
if we manage to make it through life
alone—there is no eternal life. Edward
and Bella wanted to be together forever.
We have all been designed with a desire
for eternal relationship. That life-giving
relationship is found in Christ alone.

Just think: God is right with you as
you walk down the hall at school. *You
are rescued from loneliness.* He shows up
at every game to cheer you on. *You are rescued from abandonment.*
He is the One who stands by your side at all times. *This* is the Savior
of the world … and He offers His unconditional love—*rescuing you
completely.* How amazing is that?

> "If Christ had not gone to
> the cross and suffered in our
> stead, the just for the unjust,
> there would not have been a
> spark of hope for us. There
> would have been a mighty
> gulf between ourselves and
> God, which no man ever
> could have passed."
> —J. C. Ryle[1]

He offers you His love and His words inside your heart, knowing
they are living and actively working on your behalf. Listen to His
promises as you read this prayer based on Psalm 139:1–18:

> *Dear God,*
>   *It amazes me that You know everything about me.*
> *You know my entire schedule every day. You know when*

my alarm goes off so early in the morning … and all the thoughts that run through my head as I start my day. You understand me. You "get" me, God—thanks!

You know what I'm about to say even before I say it; You know me that well! It's hard for me to even understand how deeply Your love and care touch my life.

No matter where I am, You are with me. There is no place I can go that You won't be with me.

You are my faithful guard. You hold me close and cover my life with Your loving embrace.

Even when I am afraid, You are with me. You are never afraid, and You give me confidence. I can rest securely with You. For You were the One who created my life. Every part of me was planned with purpose. I was a dream in Your heart, and You gave that dream a heartbeat.

You were with me before I was born. Oh, I thank You for creating me with Your own hands. All the love and care You took in creating my life—I must be special to You!

You rejoiced when I arrived. I was the secret inside that You introduced to the world. Thanks, Lord, for celebrating my life!

There are many other messages of love and rescue given to you through God's Word, the Bible. Look at these words to see how very special you are to Him:

> GOD, your God, chose you out of all the
> people on Earth for himself as a cherished,
> personal treasure. GOD wasn't attracted to you
> and didn't choose you because you were big
> and important—the fact is, there was almost
> nothing to you. He did it out of sheer love.
> *(Deut. 7:6–8 MSG)*

INVITATION OF A LIFETIME

I want to tell you more about the great love of Jesus Christ. His life was sacrificed to rescue yours. It reminds me of Jeremiah 1:19 (NIV), where God is speaking to Jeremiah (and to us today):

> "They will fight against you but will not
> overcome you, for I am with you and
> will rescue you," declares the LORD.

God wants to walk with you. He's committed to you. He wanted this so badly that He gave His Son to be born, live here on this earth, die for you, and now to live here with you.

He wants to live inside your life. Yes, He wants to be that close! All you have to do is ask Him to come into your heart—into your life. You can do that right now. It's not scary or weird. You don't have to get down on your knees or crouch down in a closet. If you've never asked Jesus into your heart—into your life—you can just talk to Him right where you are and pray a simple prayer like this one:

Dear Jesus, I need You. I know I am a sinner and I don't deserve Your love. But I thank You for the greatest gift You have given through Your sacrifice on the cross.

I've done many things in my life that have not pleased You. I'm so sorry. Thank You for still loving me, and, Jesus, please forgive me. Thank You for offering me hope, a new beginning, and Your never-ending love. Jesus, please come into my heart and life and be my personal Lord and Savior. Thank You for loving me and for asking me to be in Your family. I love You and am excited to live the rest of my life with You. In Your precious name, Amen.

Maybe you've just prayed this prayer for the first time. Maybe you accepted Him a long time ago, but you've never been sure of your relationship with God. Whatever the case, *now you can be.* Those are great words to hear, aren't they? Becoming a part of God's family is the best decision you will ever make. I'm so excited for you!

Through these pages, I'm sending you a huge hug. If you've just accepted Him, I want to welcome you into the

> "For God loved the world so much that he gave his one and only Son, so that everyone who believes in him will not perish but have eternal life."—John 3:16 (NLT)

family of God as my sweet sister. How very much your Abba Daddy loves you—yes, you! You are adopted into His family, and you are His very own! Satan no longer has a claim over you, and you can be free from a lifestyle of sin now. You are forgiven and free!

It's my prayer that you will come to know God's great love deeply. I can't wait to share more of His heart for you.

A MESSAGE FROM HIS HEART

So we have this amazing heavenly Father, this Savior—the True Rescuer of our lives. He gave His life for us. Day by day, we learn to trust His messages of love. As we do, we see more and more of the heart of our Hero.

He created you in beauty and strength. He rescued you in love. He speaks these words over your life.

We can rejoice, too, when we run into problems and trials, for we know that they are good for us—they help us learn to endure. And endurance develops strength of character in us, and character strengthens our confident expectation of salvation.

> And this hope will not lead to disappointment.
> For we know how dearly God loves us,
> because he has given us the Holy Spirit
> to fill our hearts with his love.
> When we were utterly helpless, Christ came at
> just the right time and died for us sinners. Now,
> most people would not be willing to die for an
> upright person, though someone might perhaps be
> willing to die for a person who is especially good.
> But God showed his great love for us by sending
> Christ to die for us while we were still sinners.
>
> *(Rom. 5:5–8 NLT)*

Just a few days ago I hung up the phone after a great conversation with my friend Rachael (from the beginning of the chapter). It has been five years since we met at the conference, and I wanted to know how she's doing. She is now nineteen, loves college, and has just declared a major—nursing. "I'm in a good place right now," she said.

After many counseling sessions and much prayer, she's beginning to heal inside. No longer is she haunted by the circumstances surrounding her birth. During our conversation she told me, "For a long time I was so afraid that part of my life would hold me back. There was a time I wanted to be the president of the United States. Would my past prevent me from going for my dreams? Now I know I wouldn't be the person I am today if this hadn't happened to me. The questions will always be there, but I know God saved me for a reason. God's given me this story, and now I want it to be shared. Maybe it can help someone."

Maybe it's been hard for you, too, to think you're special in any way—let alone God's gift. But know that you are. Know that God *says* that's who you are! Listen to these words from Him to you:

> Before I shaped you in the womb, I knew
> all about you. Before you saw the light
> of day, I had holy plans for you.
>
> *(Jer. 1:5 MSG)*

There is not a life created that is an accident. Our lives have great purpose. Yes ... *your life* is valued by Him. Think about that!

Rachael listened to words like these at the conference and wondered if this Rescuer was truly speaking these words

✛ There is not a life created that is an accident. Our lives have great purpose. Yes ... *your life* is valued by Him. Think about that! ✛

to her. Yes, He was, and He speaks them to you today. Your tiny little being was His creation, so your life was His from the start. From your conception, the Spirit of God delighted in you. He was there to make sure you would know His love. He was there to speak over your beginning and declare it beautiful. He smiled and gave His dream (you) life!

Just think, you have been carefully formed and cared for every second of your life; that's how much He cares about you.

What a faithful Father and Friend He is to us. He loved us before we even knew love ourselves. He rescues us from situations we could never escape on our own. He is our Ultimate Hero!

About three things you can be absolutely positive:
First, *every girl longs to be loved*
with a vast and endless passion.
Second, *there is a fiercely protective*
Immortal Hero who longs for your heart.
And third, *He loves you with an*
unconditional and irrevocable love.

CHAPTER 7

Flirting with Shadows

Don't lazily slip back into those old grooves of evil,
doing just what you feel like doing. You didn't
know any better then; you do now. As obedient
children, let yourselves be pulled into a way of life
shaped by God's life, a life energetic and blazing
with holiness. God said, "I am holy; you be holy."

(1 Peter 1:14–16 MSG)

Sophie found herself staring out her kitchen window at her ex-boyfriend's home. Every time she saw his house, painful memories came flooding back. It was impossible to forget the relationship because she faced a daily reminder.

Sophie was desperate for a love that would leave no scars or pain behind. She was desperate for someone who would protect, respect, and honor her. She longed, as she put it, for her "very own Edward" with all the compassion and attentiveness he would offer.

A few days later, she received a Facebook message from Brandon. His persuasive words drew her back to when she was with him ... not great moments in her life. Not moments she was proud of. Shadows in her past came creeping back.

Sophie was drawn to respond to Brandon. She tried to resist the urge to reconnect, but her emotions tempted her to relive the moments in her mind.

The dark and painful memories Sophie faced were just shadows now, but they seemed so real. In came fear, and depression soon followed.

THE BATTLE CONTINUES

What do you do in a situation like this one—when you have to face your past in a very literal way? No matter how far you've come, it's a difficult reminder of where you've been. Despite our identity in Christ and assurance of eternal victory at the end, the daily battle continues.

Remember these words from the apostle Paul, which were true in Sophie's life as well:

> I do not understand what I do…. I know that nothing good lives in me, that is, in my sinful nature. For I have the desire to do what is good, but I cannot carry it out. For what I do is not the good I want to do; no, the evil I do not want to do—this I keep on doing.
>
> *(Rom. 7:15, 18–19 NIV)*

Shame

a painful emotion caused by consciousness of guilt, shortcoming, or impropriety; something that brings censure or reproach; something to be regretted; pity
—Merriam-Webster OnLine

Think about that one. We do the things we hate and hate the things we do. For Sophie, this meant being drawn emotionally back in time to that relationship. Despite experiencing God's miraculous forgiveness and determining to move past the pain, Sophie continued to struggle.

Yes, Sophie had asked Jesus' forgiveness at the conference—and it was freely given. That's what redemption is all about! She was redeemed by Him: her sins covered by His work on the cross, her life granted a new beginning. I know—I was with her when she talked to God about it!

But it had been a while since that experience, and she was home now. Every day she encountered the Vampire's attempts to deceive her and pull her away from the freedom she found in Christ.

The True Hero offers a depth of love and connection that Sophie didn't understand. He possesses the solace and comfort she was desperate to receive. I have heard many stories similar to Sophie's—girls hurting from the past and desperate for hope. Maybe you are at that very place.

> ✝ You are forgiven. God not only wants to move you; He waits to embrace you! ✝

Know this: You are forgiven. God not only wants to move you; He waits to embrace you! His desire is for your freedom, whereas the Vampire's only desire is to assault. I know that sounds pretty rough, but truly, he has nothing good to offer your life. He desires to control, targeting your mind specifically. It's a kind of emotional game that the Vampire tries to play with your heart. I don't like that. We've already talked about how we can fight back when the Vampire tries to destroy us, but how do we move past his hurtful schemes?

PLAYING THE GAME

Over the years, many girls have told me they want to make the right choices—to move past certain things in their lives. However, I'm not sure they really want true change.

Change takes effort. Change is hard. It seems easier to just "play the game."

Unfortunately, here's what happens. You start out by just *flirting* with something you shouldn't be involved with. You think, *Why not? It doesn't seem too dangerous.* In that moment, you choose to buy into a lie that says, "Being involved in things that hurt the heart of God is not a big deal."

You go along with this until you're caught and surrounded by consequences you never thought would show up. Sadly, those consequences often lead to regret, which is then followed by shame.

In the darkness, surrounded by "yuck," we often find ourselves consumed. We feel weak and incapable. The Vampire delights in this misdirected focus. Once he has our attention, he pours on the guilt.

Shame is an interesting emotion. If allowed, it can totally take over your thoughts and paralyze your ability to move on. But that isn't your only option! That is, not unless you choose to let it be.

You see, shame can work in two very different ways. The first is to remain in your life and discolor your world by constantly reminding you of the poor choices you made or the circumstances that brought you to this point. When shame is allowed to work this way in your life, you're miserable and overwhelmed by negative thoughts and feelings.

Sound familiar? After a while you begin to feel almost numb inside—not a fun place to be. You may try to create a protective shield, but hiding behind all that shame just brings more pain.

But there's an alternative. You see, the other way shame works is to actually push you *toward God*. Did you catch that? The shame you feel can actually help you draw closer to God! It really can.

Here's how it works. Shame puts you in such a vulnerable spot that you finally understand that all you have is Him. You realize it's only through His life—through the pain He endured and the complete forgiveness He provides—that you can move on.

> "All healing is first a healing of the heart."
> —Carl Townsend, *In Pursuit of Healing*

Stepping away from regret and shame is possible through the sacrifice Christ already made for you. But you must get up, take His hand, and obediently walk with Him.

It's not easy. Moving beyond shame to make the right choices takes sacrifice and a willingness to follow through with what God asks. It's your choice. Are you going to look to God or try to handle it all on your own?

I can tell you from experience that obeying God is so worth it in the end! Sadly, however, we don't always see life's big picture and willingly do what it takes to draw close to Him. Have you experienced this before? It can be tempting to remain right where you are.

> "Although the world is full of suffering, it is full also of the overcoming of it."
> —Helen Keller, *Optimism*

Just breathe ...

Why stand still in this life? Sometimes if we don't see any hope ahead we give up. Don't do it. There's Someone to hold on to. Grab your Bible and read Psalm 46:1–4.

HOLD ON TIGHT

It's going to take more than just your efforts to keep moving past the struggles. You'll need His words and His leading in your life.

When I'm struggling, 1 Corinthians 10:13 (MSG) encourages me. I think it will help you, too:

> No test or temptation that comes your way
> is beyond the course of what others have had
> to face. All you need to remember is that
> God will never let you down; he'll never let
> you be pushed past your limit; he'll always
> be there to help you come through it.

I love that. He doesn't eliminate the struggle from our lives. Instead, He gives us powerful incentives to choose to hold very tightly to what is *good!* He provides an escape.

> There is now no condemnation [no shame]
> for those who are in Christ Jesus, because
> through Christ Jesus the law of the Spirit of life
> set me free from the law of sin and death.
> *(Rom. 8:1–2 NIV)*

Whew … what an awesome gift! It's because of Jesus' sacrifice and forgiveness that you can be set free from regret and shame. He wants you to move past them!

Maybe you have no desire or inspiration to move forward. No matter your situation, please believe there is a way forward: with Him.

I know it might seem crazy to think He'd make this offer—this chance for a new beginning—but He already has. It's one more amazing proof of the powerful love God has for you.

So when you're ready, He's there. He's there to hear your heart.

SET FREE

I am reminded of the amazing story in John 8:3–11 (NIV), where Christ reached out to the woman who had been accused by Pharisee leaders of adultery and condemned to die.

> The teachers of the law and the Pharisees brought in a woman caught in adultery. They made her stand before the group and said to Jesus, "Teacher, this woman was caught in the act of adultery. In the Law Moses commanded us to stone such women. Now what do you say?" They were using this question as a trap, in order to have a basis for accusing him.

> But Jesus bent down and started to write on the ground with his finger. When they kept on questioning him, he straightened up and said to them, "If any one of you is without sin, let him be the first to throw a stone at her." Again he stooped down and wrote on the ground.

> At this, those who heard began to go away one at a time, the older ones first, until only Jesus was left, with the woman still standing there.

> Jesus straightened up and asked her, "Woman, where are they? Has no one condemned you?"
>
> "No one, sir," she said.
>
> "Then neither do I condemn you," Jesus declared. "Go now and leave your life of sin."

The way Christ responded to this woman is incredible to me. He saw the heart of what was going on.

Those Pharisees—so filled with sin in their own lives—were declaring her sins shameful and ordering she be stoned. She *had sinned*. But Christ saw the woman, compassionately forgave, and saved her life that day.

Her Hero forgave her of the sin she had found so addicting. He demonstrated to her—and to us—what *redeemed* means: to be given a new beginning.

To restore someone's reputation and respect is something only He can do. That woman had been separated from the respectable in her society—she was an outcast. Then Jesus spoke, and from that day forward she was chosen by Him and loved purely. What an example of a True Hero!

> ✝ "Then neither do I condemn you," Jesus declared. "Go now and leave your life of sin." (John 8:11 NIV) ✝

I picture her questioning gaze of unbelief as she looked up at Jesus. I imagine the surprise, relief, absolute dedication, and devoted love she must have felt for Jesus after that day.

Jesus, because of who He is, had the ability to bring her into a life of acceptance and worth. He released her from her past. And He wants to do the same for you and me today.

Just breathe ...

What if I told you that you could walk away from every bit of shame? What if you could trade it up for peace and freedom to be who God has made you to be? *You can.* Read His words for you in Romans 8:1.

BREAKING OLD TIES

You've asked for His help and received His forgiveness. Now it's time to begin the process of breaking away from things that pull you back down. Whether it's a guy, a habit, or a thought pattern, breaking away from sin and staying free of it is the hardest part of all.

You know what you chose to do was for the best, but now temptation is staring you in the face, as it was with Sophie. Those temptations will continue. It's what you do with the thoughts when they recur—those shadows as they resurface—that will determine the outcome.

Maybe on day one you feel relief. By day two you're thankful ... but by day three, you begin to wonder if the fears and difficult thoughts will reappear. They will.

Maybe it feels impossible to completely break away from the past because it involves so much of what's around you or so much of what can so easily enter into your mind. For Sophie, it was a visual reminder of the past that was so difficult deal with. For you, it may be something different. Maybe it's your thoughts—those reminders inside that continue to resurface. Just remember who has forgiven you. Many times we are tempted to forget who we are and to whom we belong.

It's during those times of struggle—when you have been forgiven, but doubt creeps in—that you must believe the darkness no longer has a claim on you. Your dark past and sinful nature are just shadows and must be cast away by the power of Christ in you.

Think about the fact that Christ is the Light of the World. His light illuminates the darkness. His light removes the shadows, no matter how strong their hold on you. And He covers you with His forgiveness—a comforting covering that you get to receive.

✛ He accepts you as His own; He invites you to walk closely with Him. All shadows, guilt, and shame are removed. ✛

He accepts you as His own; He invites you to walk closely with Him. All shadows, guilt, and shame are removed.

HIS WORD FOR YOU

You may be thinking, *But what exactly am I supposed to do? Believe that God can change things and then it will all just suddenly be different?* Thankfully, God gives specific instruction and hope regarding those questions.

> Do not let sin control the way you live;
> do not give in to sinful desires. Do not
> let any part of your body become an
> instrument of evil to serve sin. Instead,

> give yourselves completely to God, for you
> were dead, but now you have new life.
>
> *(Rom. 6:12–13 NLT)*

Did you catch that? You are to give yourself completely to God. Will that be difficult to do? Absolutely. And you may be wondering if God will be there for you when you do fall … again. Yes. He promises us His unconditional love, and that includes when we fail. But we are given the choice to live free from sin. Live the life God offers you!

He continues:

> So use your whole body as an instrument to
> do what is right for the glory of God. Sin is
> no longer your master, for you no longer live
> under the requirements of the law. Instead,
> you live under the freedom of God's grace.
>
> *(Rom. 6:13–14 NLT)*

"Sin is no longer your master." Think about that precious woman in John 8 who was given a new reputation because of His forgiveness. Sin no longer controlled her life or her future.

Whatever your sin is, you know and God knows. Ask Him to show you how to live in freedom … specifically for you.

Just breathe …

Read Hebrews 12:1–3 and ask God to show you the things to "throw off." Why stay entangled when you have an amazing race to run!

There may be tough choices to make that seem pretty crazy even to think about. But in the midst of it all, He is with you. He's waiting to pick you up and surround you with His love!

> If we confess our sins, he is faithful and
> just and will forgive us our sins and
> purify us from all unrighteousness.
>
> *(1 John 1:9 NIV)*

STAND STRONG

Christ gives you everything you need to be strong. It's in His mighty power that we can resist the temptations and fears that the Vampire offers us. So take His strong words in Ephesians 6:10–20 and realize there is a battle so much greater than what you and I can see.

> Finally, be strong in the Lord and in His mighty
> power. Put on the full armor of God so that you
> can take your stand against the devil's schemes.
> For our struggle is not against flesh and blood, but
> against the rulers, against the authorities, against
> the powers of this dark world and against the
> spiritual forces of evil in the heavenly realms."
>
> *(Eph. 6:10–12 NIV)*

Today I want to be strong in You, God, and in the strength You give. I am nothing without You. I need

You. Having Your guard of protection over my life is the only way I'll be able to stand and turn away the Enemy. I want to stand strong.

I put on the belt of truth. I need Your truth when I am so surrounded by the lies in this world. I want to be ready and committed to fight the battles by listening for Your voice. I know Your voice is the truth.

Next I put on the breastplate of righteousness. I don't want my mind and heart to be manipulated. I want to make right choices, but that can be so difficult. I can't live a life that is holy and pure without You showing me how, God. Thanks for being with me.

I need my feet fitted with readiness. I need my life protected by my living God. Please go before me, preparing my steps as I walk through my day with Your peace. You are faithful to provide peace for my life as I read Your words and receive Your wisdom. I need Your words to be the words that I listen to.

Next I put on the shield of faith, which will help deflect the fiery darts of temptation that come my way. There are so many out there, God. I believe You have a work to complete in my life.

I put on the helmet of salvation. I am thankful that I can be so assured of heaven one day … because of You, Jesus! You are preparing my home there. For now, let me please You here.

Finally, I put on the sword of the Spirit, which is Your Word (the Word of God). I want to learn how You speak through the Bible about what I am facing right now.

Thank You for all You've given me through Your words. They bring light to me in this dark world. You are with me to protect and shield my life. I love You and thank You for filling my life with power and love through Your Holy Spirit. Thank You for the promise of Your presence.

I pray all these things in Your precious name! Amen.

CHAPTER 8
Illuminated Within

This is the message we have heard from
him and declare to you: God is light;
in him there is no darkness at all.

(1 John 1:5 NIV)

Zoe sat toward the back of the room, her head down and her eyes
snatching quick glances of me throughout the session. My heart was
drawn to her. I could tell there was so much hurt inside just by the
way she tried to blend in to the groups of girls after the sessions,
steering away from me when I attempted to connect. No eye contact.
No conversation. It was like she was hiding something, or maybe
nervous that she'd give something away. Perhaps there were secrets
she had told no one.

It takes bravery to break free of a life filled with enticement and
darkness and to walk into the light. To be exposed to God's light is
illuminating—it means our flaws are in full view. We are seen for
who we are: naked and ashamed, without the mask and the cloak we
have grown so accustomed to wearing that covers up our mess.

You may think that stepping into the light will bring intimidation, fear, vulnerability, and shame. But I guarantee you'll find it instead to be a refuge—a haven, a home. It holds comfort, safety, and the peace you long for when you're free to be who you truly are, who you were created to be.

> In God's light we are exposed, much like how, in the sunlight, *Twilight's* vampires are exposed for who they are, as Bella discovered in *Twilight:* "Edward in the sunlight was shocking. I couldn't get used to it, though I'd been staring at him all afternoon."

Zoe didn't know this refuge; she didn't have that peace. She had not been exposed to the transforming power of God's pure illumination … and it showed.

THE CONTRAST

It's incredible to think about how God's pure illumination stands in such contrast to the mirage of evil and all its deceptions. J. J. Dewey is quoted as saying, "When a light is turned on in the darkness the darkness is no more. Darkness cannot extinguish light, but light can cause darkness to immediately disappear."[1]

I love it. There is a command that physical light has over darkness. This is also so true of Christ, the Light of the World. Darkness holds life-sucking fear, the unknown camouflaged as mystery. The light of Christ illuminates the darkness—removes fear and the unknown, replaces it with peace

> "Light is that which reveals (or that which is visible) and dark is that which hides."
> —J. J. Dewey[2]

and life-giving direction. And isn't that what we want for our lives? It's what we all need!

There is nothing good about deception. No one likes the idea of being tricked or lured by evil. But when we turn to God for comfort and guidance, evil is brought out of the shadows in our lives and illuminated by the light. We are rescued from deception and given the power of God's truth instead.

Isn't that just like our God—to design such disparity between darkness and light? Just think about bright stars set against the backdrop of a night sky. This parallels spiritual darkness and the illuminating power of Christ, the Light of the World.

Let's look beyond the literal contrast of light and darkness and see how the deeper meaning daily affects our lives. The power that darkness holds in our

> "You can shine a light and dispel darkness, but you cannot shine "dark" and dispel light."—J. J. Dewey[3]

lives can consume our world. But then look at the power of darkness compared to Christ, who is the light of life!

"Living in the light" provides us with identity in the family of God, freedom from the hold of the Vampire, beauty of Christ within, direction for the daily steps, and focus on a blessed future.

> Darkness (also called "light-lessness") is by definition the absence of light.[4] Light is "something that makes things visible or affords illumination; all colors depend on light."[5]

Darkness. You can probably relate to those little-girl feelings inside of being afraid of the dark. It was the unknown that you feared, wasn't it? That insecurity of not feeling safe. Those fears told you there might be danger, that something just might jump out at any moment. You probably needed the comfort of the night-light, your teddy bear, or a hug to assure you of your safety.

Today you may not deal with the same fears, but darkness still threatens, and you still find yourself afraid.

Light. God was the One who said in the beginning, "Let there be light" (Gen 1:3 NIV) He dispensed the darkness with His words! And He can dispense the darkness in your life, too.

You see, God isn't just associated with light; He is Light Himself.

God has many things to say about light in His Word. Did you know there are twenty-seven references to light mentioned in the concordance of my Bible alone? I was amazed to see how many times He speaks of light in His Word—it must be that important to Him. Let's look at a few.

- *In John 8:12, He says, "I am the light of the world" (NIV) Christ is the Light; in Him we find security and peace.*

- *He wraps Himself in light (Ps. 104:2).*

- *He created light. When God created light, He separated light from darkness (Gen. 1:3–4). That's pretty amazing and revealing!*

- *In 1 John 1:5 it says, "God is light; in him there is no darkness at all" (NIV).*

- *I love this one: "The unfolding of your words gives light" (Ps. 119:130 NIV). So God not only is the Light; He gives light—which is life-giving to us.*

- *1 John 1:7 says, "If we walk in the light, as he is in the light, we have fellowship with one another, and the blood of Jesus, his Son, purifies us from all sin"*

(NIV). We can walk with Him in the light. We can be freed from the darkness.

There is simply no doubt that walking with Christ, in the light, illuminates our lives like nothing else. When we are His, the brilliance of Christ's light of life shines brightly from our lives.

Just breathe …

Stepping into the light at this moment, revealing all your sins and flaws, seems quite intimidating, doesn't it? What would it be like to step into the light and have Christ's light shining out of you instead? You might have been prepared for embarrassment—but instead Christ covers every hint of those feelings inside. Would you feel overwhelmed with love and gratefulness?

So what does this look like in our lives? Because He is pure light, it means our sins are visible. We're naked before Him—He sees everything. We are totally vulnerable. That can seem uncomfortable … until we realize how much we can trust Him.

We can relax, knowing our Hero accepts our flawed selves—and He forgives. Fully, completely, and forever. "He is so rich in kindness and grace that he purchased our freedom with the blood of his Son and forgave our sins. He has showered his kindness on us, along with all wisdom and understanding" (Eph. 1:7–8 NLT).

✝ We can relax, knowing our Hero accepts our flawed selves—and He forgives. Fully, completely, and forever. ✝

DARKNESS REVEALED

There is an emotionally intense scene in *Twilight* where Edward stands behind Bella in the middle of a dark forest and asks her what she thinks he really is.

"Say it," Edward says. "Out loud, say it."

Bella says in a low voice, "A vampire."

"Are you afraid?" Edward asks her.

A look of wonder crosses Bella's face. She answers truthfully: "No."

While watching that scene in the movie, I realized that Bella's powerful connection with Edward pushed her right past any fear inside. She stood unafraid, yet vulnerable. Bella was staring directly at a vampire who, minus Edward's superhuman self-control, would have taken her life.

This was incredible to me, because by his own admission, Edward is a *vampire*. He and his entire family, in fact—all of them are vampires. Now, what sets the Cullen family apart from other vampires is their choice to restrain from harming humans. Years earlier they made an admirable choice to resist their bloodlust and feed on animals instead.

But "vegetarian" or not, Edward is the feared creature. A killer, he admits. He even calls himself a monster. Throughout the series, his innate vampire nature battles his desire to do right, to protect and love Bella.

Something else that's fascinating about Edward is that he and his family don't like to go outside when the sun is shining. When they're exposed to the sun, their skin shimmers like diamonds, revealing that they are vampires. Again, an illusion of light when inside there is darkness. There's that same battle going on inside.

A lot of spiritual questions are raised in *Twilight:* Do vampires have souls? What happens if/when they finally die? Where do they go? The characters question this a great deal, leaving readers with questioning thoughts as well, maybe even about their own spiritual lives.

Uncertainty can lead to confusion—much like walking around in the dark. Think about it. If you have to feel your way around in the dark, it means

> ✝ He lights the way and reveals Truth for what it is. ✝

you're unfamiliar with your surroundings. You're likely to trip and fall. There's a good chance you'll get hurt.

But questioning can also lead to the Truth of Christ, which illuminates that darkness. In Him, we don't have to be confused. We know exactly where we're going; He lights the way and reveals Truth for what it is.

> When Jesus spoke again to the people,
> he said, "I am the light of the world.
> Whoever follows me will never walk in
> darkness, but will have the light of life."
>
> *(John 8:12 NIV)*

DRAWN TO THE STORY

Late one night following a conference session, I asked several groups of girls to hang out and talk. I wanted to hear their take on *Twilight*. What was it that so drew them into the story—that captured their attention and generated so much discussion?

We ended up chatting for hours. In the end, we weren't even

talking about the movie or the books anymore. Our conversation had gradually shifted to talking through what was going on inside.

A lot of things came up during that conversation. We talked about guys ... our hearts ... deep hurts ... what we really think about ourselves ... struggles with weight ... being misunderstood. We prayed together. We were real with each other, and it was good.

But something in particular that we talked about that night really stood out to me and started me thinking. Here's the gist of it....

In essence, we are torn. We're caught between a desire for life that is lit up, godly, whole, and clean, and a desire to stay trapped in the darkness that has become so familiar. It can be confusing!

Sometimes we find ourselves in this difficult place—in a mirage, so to speak. A mirage is an illusion. You think you see something that in actuality is not there. Like those movie scenes of guys in the desert looking out into the distance, so desperately in need of water that their minds play tricks on them. They think they see an oasis just beyond the horizon ... when truly there is no water at all.

The same is true for us today. When we're caught up in a mirage, we can't think beyond it. It captures our attention; we're trapped and blinded to reality. So our desire to live in the light of Christ—with Him, for Him, to please Him—*has* to be stronger than our drive toward the dark.

✠ Christ provides us with everything we are longing for and all that can't be found anywhere else. ✠

If we could just grasp the concept that in Christ we are His! In Him we don't have to remain hidden in darkness, fear, and regret. In Christ, in His words, *truths* are revealed to us. In Him we belong.

We have His protection and safety; our destiny is sealed. He provides separation from the darkness through His work on the cross. Through Christ's sacrifice, His blood becomes our covering; it is our protection and shield. Christ provides us with everything we are longing for and all that can't be found anywhere else.

ZOE'S STORY

After one of my conference sessions, Zoe quietly approached me. In my heart I thanked God for this opportunity, and we found a place to talk.

She began sharing, piece by piece, about her incredibly difficult life. I can't forget the sound of her quiet voice, nor the way her hair was draped in front of her face in an effort to hide the tears.

I had watched Zoe all weekend, and I wasn't sure if that "wall of protection" she had built around herself would fall. She had looked so sad and alone. But now here I was, hearing her story and understanding why. We talked and talked. Then we prayed. She was desperate for help, and she was surrounded by so many who were praying for a breakthrough. God worked deeply inside her.

The next day, I saw a new confidence as she walked into the room. Her facial expression had changed. There was a brightness in her eyes. She wasn't hidden in the dark shadows of the room anymore—it was like she was lit up inside. I watched conversations happening between her and other girls. It was obvious that something was different.

I knew it wasn't something I could have done. There were too many things shared that would take time and healing. Only the

Holy Spirit could break through her darkness in such an immediate way … *and He did!* She had been given tangible, living hope.

What I saw that day was God's Spirit working through Zoe. He heard her heart, and He comforted her. Romans 12:2 says, "Do not conform any longer to the pattern of this world, but *be transformed by the renewing of your mind.* Then you will be able to test and approve what God's will is—his good, pleasing and perfect will" (NIV). This kind of transformation begins when we cast our cares on Him. It's illumination in the purest form.

Because of God's power at work in her heart, Zoe didn't need to be afraid. Psalm 27:1 tells us so: "The LORD is my light and my salvation—whom shall I fear? The LORD is the stronghold of my life—of whom shall I be afraid?" (NIV).

Looking back on that day, I thank God for the hope He gave Zoe … and I thank Him for you. He can deliver the same hope and healing to your life at this moment. He really can.

Maybe you have a dark area in your life that you have shared with no one. You might be desperate for the light of Christ but unsure what to do next. The great news is that Christ is there to lead you forward. His words are true and His love is secure. If you let Him, He can begin to illuminate that darkness and light the way.

Just breathe …

Look at His words in 1 Peter 2:9—God declares who you are. He wants you to be freed from the darkness and all it brings with it! He has an amazing life for you to live in Him. You can trust Him. Take His hand and move forward.

> And so we know and rely on the love God
> has for us. God is love. Whoever lives in
> love lives in God, and God in him.
>
> *(1 John 4:16 NIV)*

Like Zoe, we are to be illuminated by Christ—rescued from the dark and all of the deception that darkness brings. And what does this illumination look like? We need to know so we can recognize it.

When God is inside your life others will recognize it, and you will know that you are powerfully loved and established in Him. Knowing this inside provides the way for you to live with purpose in your life. Life in Christ is the answer to what so many are looking for today. He can provide the comfort, safety, and security you long for.

✚ **Life in Christ is the answer to what so many are looking for today. He can provide the comfort, safety, and security you long for.** ✚

Just look at these promises from the heart of your Hero:

- *He offers you hope.* Message: "You belong." You have a home in Christ, giving you security, a future, and family. You have the hope of life with Him—and eternal life and love in your future. "May integrity and uprightness protect me, because my hope is in you" (Ps. 25:21 NIV).
- *He offers you the promise of family heritage in Him.* Message: "You are valued." You have a fiercely protective, adoring Father who never leaves you. You are accepted—adopted into His family just as you are. You

have an everlasting Father. "Your statutes are my heritage forever; they are the joy of my heart" (Ps. 119:111 NIV).

- *He offers you the gift of salvation.* Message: "You are loved." You have an unconditional, eternally loving Savior in Christ, the true Immortal Hero. You are rescued from the entrapments of the Vampire to enjoy lasting peace and unfailing love. "For God so loved the world that he gave his one and only Son, that whoever believes in him shall not perish but have eternal life" (John 3:16 NIV).

PART III

Mystery Embraced

Because of your faithfulness, bring me
out of this distress. In your unfailing
love, silence all my enemies and destroy
all my foes, for I am your servant.

(Ps. 143:11–12 NLT)

CHAPTER 9
Living Brave and Beautiful

Commit your way to the LORD; trust in
him and he will do this: He will make your
righteousness shine like the dawn, the justice
of your cause like the noonday sun.

(Ps. 37:5–6 NIV)

Opening scene. Words could not express the pain and heartbreak felt that day. In a moment, their entire worlds had changed. The death of Ruth's husband—and for Naomi, the death of her husband and sons—was almost more than each could bear.

Ruth had lost everything she knew—her husband, their home, and the hope of a family together. Tears streamed down her face as emptiness, abandonment, and extreme loss consumed her.

A voice inside urged her to stay close to Naomi, but that would mean giving up her homeland and starting over in a new place. The easiest thing now would be to return home, settle down, and marry again.

But for Ruth there was no other choice. Her heart's desire to be devoted to Naomi was stronger than the urge inside her to leave.

Just breathe …

Maybe you have read this inspiring story. If not, look
up the book of Ruth in the Old Testament! We see
Ruth's amazing loyalty and compassion. Do you think
in the midst of it all she also struggled with fear and
discouragement? It would have been tough for anyone.
How would you have felt in her situation?

Though she was desperate and afraid, Ruth's faith kept her going.
"Where you go I will go," she said passionately, lunging forward and
clinging tightly to Naomi (Ruth 1:16 NIV). With that promise, she
committed to following her mother-in-law into a place of unseen
outcomes and circumstances.

"But Ruth replied, 'Don't ask
me to leave you and turn
back. Wherever you go, I will
go; wherever you live, I will
live. Your people will be my
people, and your God will be
my God.'"—Ruth 1:16 (NLT)

And so the two journeyed to
Bethlehem as the barley harvest was
beginning. Their plan was to find
enough leftover grain from the fields
to fill their hungry bellies. "Do the
next thing," they would tell them-
selves. Day by day they trusted God to provide. And He did!

What a story! We see a young woman bravely turn from extremely
difficult emotions and choose to adopt Naomi's customs, her land,
and her God. And God blessed her! God directed Ruth's life in order
to provide her rescue.

Just breathe …

I love that—He provided her rescue. Did you know there
is a love story in the book of Ruth? It gets even better.

Grab a cup of hot chocolate or coffee, and let's keep reading.

Scene two. Sweat dripped from Ruth's brow as she picked wheat and barley morsels out of her hair. There was nothing attractive about her at the moment—or so she thought.

The owner of the field, Boaz, had the self-possessed swagger of any sought-after, intelligent, rich young man. But he was also generous and loving, and he had compassion for Ruth's situation. Her radiance drew him to her; he could not take his eyes off of this beautiful woman.

Ruth ignored the flirtatious gestures from the harvesters of the field, but she could not ignore Boaz. Something about his gaze told Ruth that he did not care about her appearance that day.

Boaz respectfully asked the harvesters about the young woman gleaning in his field. He learned all the details of her recent journey from Moab and her decision to stand by Naomi after their husbands' deaths.

Boaz saw beyond Ruth's appearance. He saw her bravery, loyalty, and persistence. She was unlike any other woman he had ever met. She had found favor in his eyes; he was captivated by her.

Just breathe …

What a story! Don't you just love the way Boaz is treating Ruth? Isn't it amazing to see guys treat girls with great respect? We don't see that very often, but I get excited to see there are guys who do!

Scene three. Eventually Boaz spoke to Ruth, letting her know that she was welcome to continue working in his fields. He showed her favor, insisting that she take more than what she needed. He invited her to join him for dinner.

Boaz was quite the gentleman. He even spoke a blessing over Ruth while talking with her: "May the LORD repay you for what you have done. May you be richly rewarded by the LORD, the God of Israel, under whose wings you have come to take refuge" (Ruth 2:12 NIV).

Ruth had to be as impressed with Boaz as he was with her. But what I think spoke most deeply to Ruth was how Boaz saw her heart. He saw the amazing girl she was, and I believe he saw his future with her.

Just breathe …

> I just got overwhelmed with the thought of my amazing husband, Tim. He is my Boaz! I thank God for my extremely handsome and incredibly devoted man. He sees my heart and loves me no matter what! Maybe one day I can share with you the story of how God brought us together—it's really cool!

Scene four. Ruth must have been excited as she went to tell Naomi about their first meeting. "He even said to me, 'Stay with my workers until they finish harvesting all my grain'" (Ruth 2:21 NIV).

Naomi urged Ruth to keep going back to Boaz's field. She also shared some surprising news: Boaz, it turned out, was a close family relative—a "kinsman-redeemer." In those days, a kinsman-redeemer was a man designated in a family to marry a young widow, carry on the family name, and take care of her property as his own.

Still fragile from the loss of her beloved husband, Ruth began to wonder if this kind man, who had treated her so respectfully, had been sent by God to restore her heart. Maybe, just maybe ... *he was the one*. Such kindness and gentle strength were qualities hard to find in a man. It was these qualities that drew her to his heart.

Scene five. Naomi urged Ruth to go meet Boaz at the threshing floor, where he was winnowing barley. Ruth once again honored Naomi by following her instructions.

Kneeling at Boaz's feet, Ruth waited respectfully for his response. Surprised but pleased, Boaz realized that this lovely woman had come to receive his blessing.

Again we see Boaz's heart as once more he spoke kindly to her. Her humble heart and reputation as a woman of noble character touched him deeply. He expressed his interest and willingness to be her kinsman-redeemer.

Just breathe ...

Don't you love this guy, Boaz? Can you imagine how Ruth must have felt to be treated with such respect and honor? Have you ever seen someone in such a relationship of respect? I hope you have. It's great to have that example in front of you. I've seen that in my parents' relationship. I pray that others can see that in my life with Tim.

Scene six. As it turned out, Boaz wasn't actually Ruth's closest relative.

And so Boaz went on a quest to find out what this other man, this kinsman-redeemer, would say. It ended up that the man chose not to purchase Naomi's land and acquire Ruth as his wife, which left Boaz next in line. Whew … she would marry her man!

You can imagine Ruth's excitement when Boaz announced his decision to purchase the land and without hesitation chose Ruth as his bride.

Just breathe …

I love to hear how Boaz sought after Ruth. His love was deep and true. What does that tell you about Boaz? What quality in Boaz do you admire the most? Take a minute and thank God for the awesome man he will bring into your life one day. Pray that He will show you the strong qualities you also deserve. Wait for him—it's worth it!

So let's look at this amazing story. Ruth was faithful to God through extremely difficult times, and He honored her life with an amazing family, greater purpose than she could imagine, and a peace in knowing she had followed her God. What a rescue story of love!

It's a powerful picture. Her heart was mended, her life restored, and her future blessed! Quite the portrait of brave and beautiful! Eventually, Ruth and Boaz had a son, whom they named Obed. He would go on to be the father of Jesse and the grandfather of King David—placing Ruth directly in the family lineage of Jesus!

> "Then I will rejoice in the LORD.… With every bone in my body I will praise him: 'LORD, who can compare with you? Who else rescues the helpless from the strong?'"—Psalm 35:9–10 (NLT)

Just breathe ...

I love to see how God orchestrated His plan to provide His blessings for Ruth—blessings that were greater than she could ever dream! It reminds me of how even when we can't see His provision, we can trust He has all things taken care of. He has the big picture in mind.

PORTRAIT OF STRENGTH

Helpless, hopeless, widowed, and childless. This is where we found Ruth at the beginning of her story. But it's hardly where she ended up. She could have given up and gone home—and there would have been a very different story. But she didn't.

There were times when it must have seemed like there was nothing in life offering her hope. Instead of giving up, she took a deep breath and made a conscious decision to hold tightly to Naomi's God—whom she was only beginning to know—and chose to follow His lead.

In Ruth's story, we get to see where she came from and where God took her. I wonder who will look back on my life and yours one day, seeing the hard times and blessings, too.

> ✝ No matter our story, God can take a painful past and transform it into a beautiful portrait. ✝

Life is filled with both. It's interesting how our lives are lived in front of a watching world. We may not think they can learn from our story, but they can. They will learn from our mistakes and desire to carry on our heart as well. No matter our story, God can take a painful past and transform it into a beautiful portrait.

I can't promise that if you follow Jesus, your life will be perfect. But it's worth it to have His cover. And I promise you this: There is peace in knowing the True Rescuer and receiving His covering. His covering makes us strong!

> The LORD hears his people when they call to
> him for help. He rescues them from all their
> troubles. The LORD is close to the brokenhearted;
> he rescues those whose spirits are crushed.
> The righteous person faces many troubles, but
> the LORD comes to the rescue each time.
>
> *(Ps. 34:17–19 NLT)*

LIVING IN BEAUTY

Living beautifully means moving from doubt and fear to discovering who you were designed to be—and then living that life without hesitation.

Sounds pretty good, doesn't it? Sounds pretty good, doesn't it? This is what my friend Renee did. I'll never forget her dance. There Renee stood, praising God with everything she had. What human eyes saw was a severely disabled young woman who had experienced extreme trauma. Her skin was terribly scarred, her body horribly disfigured. Renee had miraculously survived a terrible accident, but the accident didn't touch the person she is inside.

What God saw, I know, was His beautiful girl. God looked at her heart and saw beauty.

I wish you could meet this amazing woman. I've never known anyone who accepted such physical disability with so much grace. Her body has endured tremendous pain. Her life has been altered in every way. Yet Renee lives life with grace and optimism. She has an inner strength and focus not her own.

What amazes me most is to see her continually encourage *others!* She doesn't allow herself to be consumed by her own physical struggles. She thinks of the needs of others despite facing pain every second of every day.

Does she sometimes still struggle inside? I'm sure she does. But she blesses those around her by keeping her focus on God. He has given her hope and a future.

> ✝ The true beauty I see in her life is beauty in its purest form—as though everything was stripped away so we could see what God has placed inside. ✝

Renee was once physically beautiful. Now she possesses something much more extraordinary for the world to see. The true beauty I see in her life is beauty in its purest form—as though everything was stripped away so we could see what God has placed inside.

Just breathe …

Ruth and Renee, women from extremely different situations, faced struggles that challenged them and made them stronger. They are both amazing women with incredible strength not their own. How did their stories inspire you?

Your struggles may be different from those faced by Renee or our Old Testament heroine, but like Ruth and Renee, your story doesn't end here.

God's design for your life is that you would be beautifully strong—strong in heart, strong in purpose, and strong in person.

When times get tough—and they do, don't they?—He doesn't expect
you to deal with life perfectly. He doesn't expect you to "toughen up."

What He wants is for your heart to be strengthened by His love.
He wants to see your life filled with His courage. You need His wisdom to know what to do next. You need it in order to find the hope
with which to hang on.

Christ tells us in 2 Corinthians 12:9, "My grace is sufficient
for you, for my power is made perfect in weakness" (NIV). In other
words, it's in our weakness that His strength is most evident. Our
weakness provides the perfect opportunity for Christ to shine. I love
that!

We find strength in God, who is so much greater than we could
ever imagine. This very different from what we hear all around us,
isn't it? So often we're told that we need to be strong in ourselves. But
the truth is, it's when we go to Him that we are beautifully strong!

That beautiful promise is in stark contrast to what the Ultimate
Vampire offers. In his story is fear, frustration, exhaustion, depression
… a cycle of dark emotions that go on and on. His view of life is the
darkness you find yourself in when you take your eyes off the Savior.

It takes a brave girl to walk out of the darkness and into the
light. But by doing this, you'll veer away from the enticements of
the Vampire and find yourself on the "higher road" of honoring God
with your life. Let's talk about what that looks like.

THE KING IS ENTHRALLED BY YOUR BEAUTY

I once heard someone say that to honor someone is to uphold her
heart, to know who that person is, and to stand by her no matter
what. How do we actually do that with God?

To first get an idea of the *why*, let's take a look at Psalm 45:11 (NIV):

> The [K]ing is enthralled by your beauty;
> honor him, for he is your [L]ord.

Did you catch what it says about honoring Him? You honor Him *because of who He is.*

You honor Him because you love Him.

He also tells you practically *how* to do this in 1 Timothy 4:12: "Don't let anyone look down on you because you are young, but set an example for the believers in speech, in life, in love, in faith and in purity" (NIV).

It's evident in your words. It's in how you live, in your attitudes, in your relationships. In the everyday moments, you make choices about all of these things. And through that example of honor, others will be drawn to the Hero.

It's like this: I'm much more peaceful when all is well between God and me. When I'm in tune with Him, my friends can tell the difference. It's all over my face, in what I say, and in how I treat others. I'm more relaxed, happy ... I'm just better.

Just breathe ...

Take a moment to ask God to show you what honoring Him would look like for your life.

Sound impossible? Remember, God isn't asking you to live a perfect life. He alone lived that. You can set your heart on doing everything possible to live for Him in each area—not because you are trying to achieve perfection, but because you love Him. In 1 John 4:19 it says, "We love because he first loved us" (NIV) Did you catch that? He loved you *first*. Focus on that. It's a great reminder of who you're honoring—and why.

FEELING FAR FROM BRAVE OR BEAUTIFUL

There's a scene in *Twilight* where Bella, afraid for her safety and desperate to escape an evil vampire, grabs her bag and jumps into her truck to head far from home. Her adventure has turned crazy! Now she's filled with fear, with nowhere to turn. She needs courage; she needs a strength not her own.

> "Don't be concerned about the outward beauty of fancy hairstyles, expensive jewelry, or beautiful clothes. You should clothe yourselves instead with the beauty that comes from within, the unfading beauty of a gentle and quiet spirit, which is so precious to God."—1 Peter 3:3–4 (NLT)

Sometimes I try to do things all on my own. It's during these times I end up most desperate for God. But in the midst of so much "yuck," I feel unworthy of His love. And yet, during these most vulnerable moments and most unlovable times, I have also felt His love reach out to me the most. I have been His little girl who is hurting inside, and He has been there to rescue my heart, giving me courage and hope to hang on.

What about you? There's probably been at least one time in your life when you've needed to be rescued. Maybe you feel trapped in a difficult relationship or a situation that seems to have no way out. Maybe you feel far from brave and beautiful. Maybe you realize your own choices are fighting against God's—and now you're stuck somewhere you don't want to be. You know you need God's help but are afraid to ask. It feels too late for change or too hard to move on.

When you are empty and without hope, it's then that you receive the courage and beauty you don't have on your own. It's then that He offers you all that He is. That's a pretty great exchange, isn't it? God takes those scars and leaves beauty in their place.

I found the perfect picture of this in Psalm 103:1–5 (MSG). These words greatly encouraged me, and I think they'll encourage you, too.

> O my soul, bless GOD. From head to toe, I'll bless
> his holy name! O my soul, bless GOD, don't forget
> a single blessing! He forgives your sins—every one.
> He heals your diseases—every one. He redeems
> you from hell—saves your life! He crowns you
> with love and mercy—a paradise crown. He wraps
> you in goodness—beauty eternal. He renews your
> youth—you're always young in his presence.

Wow. Look at God's words for you: He forgives, He heals, He redeems, He crowns you with love and mercy, He renews your life. What a story of beauty and courage! What a beautiful portrait!

It's a miracle, really. And it can happen inside your life!

A BRAVE QUESTION

A girl named Katrina once approached me after a conference and asked, "Okay, I know this is a stupid question, but am I just supposed to go home and be different?"

It wasn't a stupid question at all; it was a brave question. And I knew exactly what Katrina meant. She wanted her life to be different—to be better. She wanted to honor God. But how?

I admired Katrina for asking what was probably on everyone's mind that day. She knew she wouldn't change just by trying to make things better. And she was right.

Bravely following Christ brings change. Change comes through what we allow Christ to do *inside us*—not by our own doing.

I once heard failure defined as "dropping down into your fears, your worst habits, your ungodly relationships, and refusing to move." It's that part about refusing to move that's so sad. I've been there. Maybe you have too.

> ✛ Change comes through what we allow Christ to do *inside us*—not by our own doing. ✛

Maybe you're tired. Maybe you're worn out from trying so hard on your own to stand up. The Vampire enjoys seeing you "locked in place." He wants you there, vulnerable and afraid, feeling stuck. This is especially when you need to cry out to God: when you don't know what to do next. It's in those times that God will meet you there. He offers comfort and escape from fear, and the reassurance of who you are and who He is. Your Hero has given you a brave spirit and matchless beauty.

I often quote Psalm 56:3 to my sons: "When I am afraid, I will trust in you" (NIV). It was part of David's prayer when he was captured by enemies. What a great reminder that there *will* be fearful times in life and that *when* you are afraid, you can trust Him.

Just breathe ...

You can just talk to God. "God, I need You. Today and each day, would You please take me by the hand? Sometimes I feel afraid and unsure of how to walk through this life. Please help me, God. I'm confused about a lot, and I need someone to lead me."

CHAPTER 10

Undying Love

This is how we know what love is: Jesus
Christ laid down his life for us. And we ought
to lay down our lives for our brothers.

(1 John 3:16 NIV)

At the core of our hearts—mine, yours, every girl you know—is the longing to be loved. Each of us is searching for a hero who is eternally attracted to, fiercely protective of, and passionately committed to us. As we discovered in our conversations about what drew us to Edward, we're all on a search for a hero who will prove his love no matter the cost.

The epic love story of Christ and His love never ends, providing the rescue our hearts need. His unrestricted love knows no boundaries. Nowhere else can we find this type of love. Yet often we keep searching.

✝ At the core of our
hearts ... is the longing
to be loved. ✝

DESPERATE SEARCH

Imagine someone on national television claiming to possess the secret to authentic love and offering information about how to attain it. Let's not even try to guess the number of consumers who would call for information.

How Kids Define Love

"When my grandmother got arthritis, she couldn't bend over and paint her toenails anymore. So my grandfather does it for her all the time, even when his hands got arthritis too. That's love."
—Rebecca, age eight

"Love is when you go out to eat and give somebody most of your French fries without making them give you any of theirs."—Chrissy, age six

"Love is when you tell a guy you like his shirt, then he wears it everyday."
—Noelle, age seven[1]

It wouldn't really matter *who* was claiming to hold the answer; there would be buyers willing to purchase products, travel to destinations around the world … whatever it took. All in a desperate search for love.

The fact is, there are thousands of images and representations of love all around us, both historically and in popular culture. You find them in song lyrics, movies, television sitcoms, commercials, Internet Web sites.… All claim to have the answers, and each points us to a different source of "lasting" love.

It's often the stories in film and in print that capture our attention and draw us in, successfully connecting in some way to our hearts. Let's look at a few prominent love stories and examine what these examples tell us about love.

1. Romeo and Juliet.

Plot. Despite family feuding (or perhaps because of it?) two young lovers plan an escape that propels them toward tragedy.

From the front matter of *New Moon:* "These violent delights have violent ends / And in their triumph die, like fire and powder, / Which, as they kiss, consume." *Romeo and Juliet,* Act II, Scene VI

This is classic "forbidden fruit" love. Both want what they cannot have. In the end, some say they died a tragic death … all in the name of love.

2. Bella and Edward.

Plot. Girl falls for boy, cautiously aware of his inherent vampire nature but willing nonetheless to give up everything to be with him forever.

In *Twilight,* Bella tells Edward, "I would rather die than stay away from you…. I'm an idiot."[2]

Let's be honest. This love is dependent. Dependent on the life of another to give what can't be offered—eternal, perfect love. We can look at Bella and Edward's relationship from every angle; we analyze every word and are captured by the hope of our own Edward-Bella story.

What is it about the story that drives and intrigues us? It's Edward's protectiveness toward Bella, his desire to understand her. These qualities capture Bella's heart and ours. It speaks to our need inside to be valued and deeply loved. But as amazing as this love may seem, it is not eternal, life-giving, or perfect.

In a recent interview, Kristen Stewart, the actress who plays the part of Bella in *Twilight,* sums up the Bella-Edward relationship this way: "He's a vampire and would suck the last bit of blood out of her, yet she's completely fascinated by him." What does that tell us about love?

3. Rose and Jack (from the movie *Titanic*).

Plot. Spoiled rich girl on the maiden voyage of a doomed ship seeks escape and rescue in the arms of a starving young artist.

Jack to Rose: "I'm not an idiot. I know how the world works. I've got ten bucks in my pocket, I have nothing to offer you and I know that…. But I'm too involved now. You jump, I jump, remember? I can't turn away without knowing you'll be all right."

Both of the characters in this story were unhappy with their lives, searching for *something* to give their existence meaning. For them, love was that "something," and it was more important to them than even life itself. Would you say they understood the true meaning of love? Why or why not?

4. Cinderella and Prince Charming.

Plot. Ill-treated stepdaughter experiences an enchanted evening at the village ball. There she meets a handsome prince, who falls crazy in love with her and searches the world over carrying her lost shoe.

As simplistic as this story may seem, many have bought into the dream of a "happily ever after story." We see it over and over in books and movies even today! Do you find yourself taken in by storybook romance?

Just breathe …

Which of these stories captures your heart? Why? Which of these heroines do you relate to the most? Why?

Why do we find ourselves so taken by forbidden love or the lesser loves in our lives? All of our human love (as good as it can be) and all of the love stories combined pale in the shadow of our Hero's love. Why do we often settle for the raindrop of love when we could have the magnificent ocean and all its billowing, crashing waves of love? Which will you choose? *I want the ocean!*

I love what Frank Viola says in his book *From Eternity to Here:* "Every love story that the minds of mortal men and women construct, every love story that has made its appearance in the pages of human history—whether fiction or nonfiction—is but a reflection, a pale image, a faint portrait, a scrambled version of the sacred romance of the ages."[3]

> "We are half-hearted creatures, fooling about with drink and sex and ambition when infinite joy is offered us, like an ignorant child who wants to go on making mud pies in a slum because he cannot imagine what is meant by the offer of a holiday at the sea. We are far too easily pleased."—C. S. Lewis, "The Weight of Glory"[4]

So what is the "sacred romance of the ages"? The true, ultimate story of love—*the perfect love of God.*

Deep within we are all so longing for love. But what is love, exactly? First John 4:16 says, "God is love. Whoever lives in love lives in God, and God in him" (NIV).

In his book *The Four Loves,* one of my favorite authors, C. S. Lewis, categorized love as "need love" (the love a child has for his mother) and "gift love" (ultimately shown by God's love for all humanity). After continual study he realized how complicated those categories are.

He then divided love into four categories, based in part on the four Greek words for love: affection, friendship, eros, and charity.

Such an interesting way to look at the many ways we love people and things in our world! You may love your best friend, you may love shopping, and you may love your family—but your love for each is on a different level.

- *Affection* (Greek word: storge). *Love through familiarity, especially among family members.*
  - *It's the kind of love that many expect simply because of the family connection and familiarity. It's not always easy to find this love in our hearts toward others, even for family. We don't have to always accept what they do, but we need to ask God to give us acceptance and love for them despite the hurts they may have caused.*

- *Friendship* (Greek word: philia). *Love between two people who share a common interest or activity.*
  - *The bond in this type of love exists not because of any characteristic in the persons, but because of the activity that is shared. We can build awesome friendships that may last a lifetime through school or sports we are involved in.*

- *Eros. Love based on "being in love" and on activities that you enjoy doing together.*
  - *This type of love is love that reaches beyond a*

friendship to dating and can apply to marriage. This is in a way "blind devotion" based on who someone is—not on what is received from him or her.

~ **Charity** *(Greek word:* agape*). According to the Bible, the greatest of the loves.*
  ~ *This love is unconditional toward one another and not dependent on anything worthy or lovable in the life of the one loved. This love gives and cares no matter what the consequence or situation.*

Just breathe ...

Think about the people you love most in your life. How would you describe the love you have for each of them?

Wow ... that last one, *agape*—a description of God's love—is so beyond our own ability! This type of love is possible only as we accept His love to then share with others. This love is the most needed of all loves and is what all the other loves flow out from.

"*Human love is limited.* It is **not** what it was originally created to be, even in the best of people and circumstances, except when Jesus Himself is loving in and through a person."[5]

Of all the stories of love we experience, we must consider the greatest epic of all:

God has authored the most incredible love story ever written. It is a story that has set the standard for all romantic literature to follow. Every great saga follows the story line of the hidden romance contained in Scripture. But none can trump it. You and I were born into such a romance, the romance of the ages.[6]

Without exception, every person longs for perfect love. When reading *Twilight* or watching the film, we long to be loved like Bella is loved by Edward. But no matter how chivalrous, how brave, how drawn he is to Bella, his love is not perfect.

"This is one of the miracles of love: It gives a power of seeing through its own enchantments and yet not being disenchanted."
—C. S. Lewis, *A Grief Observed*

Longing for love is not wrong. But think about this: There is only one source of perfect love—Christ. God created a place inside each of us that can be filled only by Christ. It can't be filled with anything less. Millions of people try every day to fill their hearts with lesser loves—but nothing else satisfies.

So sit back and take this in: You are free to stop filling your empty spaces inside with lesser things, with less than God's love.

HIS WORDS: POETRY

I was sharing with a girl after a conference session about how much God loves her. I could see in her face that she desperately wanted to believe but couldn't accept the words as truth. Her heart had been very recently crushed, and thoughts of love seemed very far away. It became so clear: *How can she understand about God's love when she has never experienced anything like it before?*

I began to share God's words on what true love looks like, reading from 1 Corinthians 13. Two to three verses into the chapter, I paused and made a comment about how I knew this was probably familiar to her, but to stay with me.

To my surprise, she was listening attentively. "Please," she said, "keep reading. I've never heard this before. It's so beautiful … it sounds like poetry."

I loved hearing that—God's love letter described as poetry! Within that chapter she heard love described in a way she never had before. She was shocked that God had such beautiful things to say about love.

Those words were new to her. *His* description of love was like a foreign language—yet His words were speaking to her heart! To be with someone who was hearing these words for the first time was a beautiful moment.

The incredible thing about 1 Corinthians 13 is that it's God's definition of love. It's not a human description of love; it is His description. It's about love that is defined and created by God.

This isn't a love we can truly wrap our arms around. In fact, it can be experienced only when it is first received by the Giver.

✚ **It's about love that is defined and created by God.** ✚

Did you catch that? *You have to receive it from God Himself in order to demonstrate it toward others.* Kind of takes the pressure off, doesn't it?

You see, perfect love belongs to God alone. By that, I mean that His standard is so high we can't achieve it on our own. Knowing this should be what drives us toward His love—a gift from the Creator Himself.

Remember when I talked about how Edward couldn't give Bella the thing she needed most? *This* is what I meant. Perfect love is the exclusive gift from the Creator of love: *Perfect love can be given only by God.* It's impossible for us to achieve on our own. Even Edward isn't capable of giving it, as devoted as he is.

But we are not without hope. The good news of the epic love story of all time is that there's a source of perfect love: God's limitless *agape* love.

THE LOVE LETTER

In 1 Corinthians 13, God shows us a picture of what love really should look like.

Just breathe …

I love the fact that we can hold our own copy of God's love letters to us. Let's look at 1 Corinthians 13 together. Feel free to underline, highlight in a fun color, or write a note alongside about the meaning it holds for you.

What if the whole world could take just a look at this? So many things would work differently if we would all believe these words as truth! Let's look at God's poetry closely from the perspective of someone who might be reading it for the first time. I've written it like a prayer, so feel free to pray this along with me.

> *"Love is patient, love is kind."*
> *God, I know everyone doesn't see love like this. I have to show patience even to those who are not patient*

and kind? That is what You're asking, isn't it? What a
tough job—to demonstrate Your love. But when I do, I
am living my life like You. This will make a difference
in my world. You've got to show me how, God. I want to
make a difference. I want to show Your love.

"It does not envy, it does not boast, it is not proud."

Wow, that's the opposite of what circles in my
head every day, God. In my world everything is com-
pared. Everyone seems to shout their greatness louder
than the next person. It's a competition, God. I don't
want to join this game. You speak Your blessing and
approval over me every moment. That's enough ... that
is true love.

"It is not rude, it is not self-seeking."

Life doesn't need to be all about me or the fight to
make it that way. It's exhausting, Lord. I've tried that.
I need another focus, God—something bigger than me.

"It is not easily angered, it keeps no record of
wrongs."

This one is tough, God. Don't we have to keep
score? You know my life, and You desire to show me how
to live it. You'll keep me focused on what is important
and what's not. You'll keep me surrounded by others who
build me up as a person, not tear me down.

"Love does not delight in evil but rejoices with the
truth."

Why is it so easy to see the payback on what has
hurt me so badly? Show me how to focus on the truth

and how to move forward—not to be caught up in the past.

"It always protects, always trusts, always hopes, always perseveres."

What an amazing gift to offer someone—what an amazing gift to receive! It's hard to imagine that type of relationship, God. To be protected, my body and heart shielded from harm. For someone to consider me of that much value—that shows respect. To be in relationship with someone I can trust with my time, my words, and my heart—that is a gift. To be shown faithfulness and to have a trust that I am secure in a relationship that will not end—that is love that perseveres.

I don't know where to find this love outside of You, God. Is that why You offer it to me? I can know Your love. I can hold it in my heart and then offer this love to others. You've got to show me how. I want to know Your love inside, and I want to show Your love to the world!

Just breathe …

There are millions of ways to share Christ's love—but in what specific way has God designed you to do that? How about speaking with respect and love to those in your world? What about compassionately listening to a hurting friend? How about giving to someone in need? Reach out to someone who is difficult to love. He'll show you how.

LONGING FOR LOVE

I know of one specific time in my life when God asked me to love someone who, in my own strength, was impossible to love. I felt in my heart there was no love to give. God asked me to picture in my mind what *He* thought about this. I felt He agreed with me. Within my heart, in my strength, there *was* nothing to give. I needed more than I had inside.

I needed a deeper love than I could conjure on my own. I needed *His love.*

God asked me to picture His face and not the face of the one who had hurt me. I needed to picture how God loved this individual first and how He was in the process of healing and working. Then, if I was willing to come alongside Christ, He would give me His love.

I got it. This love—God's love—could reach the difficult spots. It would be *His love,* not my own, that could break through and love in a way that was needed.

On my own, I couldn't give that … but *He* could. That day I saw a glimpse of *agape* love up close.

When we love someone with *agape* love, we love out of *His love.* It's this love that we all need—this love that is greater than any other. It's this love that takes true surrender and sacrifice. Christ—our Immortal Hero—already offers that.

God talks about this perfect love in 1 John 4:18: "There is no fear in love. But perfect love drives out fear" (NIV).

We often live in fear instead of in His love. Think about how the Vampire weaves his lies into the pattern of our thoughts for so long. We hear his words in our minds over and over again. We begin to believe them … even his definition of love itself. It takes God's truth—His words—to cut through these thoughts of ours and distinguish what is truth and what is not.

God calls us to love as He loves. But think how impossible that is outside of Him. It's true! We must draw closer to Him in order to be like Him. In order to love like He loves.

Think about these words again—and I promise you they can be life changing: Until you understand the amazing, unconditional, without-end love of God, you can't possibly receive it or give it away. "We love because he first loved us" (1 John 4:19 NIV). He chose us *first*. Think about that one. It's a powerful truth!

Thank You, God, for a picture of love like none in this world. Thank You for the gift of Your Son—the perfect demonstration of what true love looks like. Thank You for giving Your Holy Spirit to live inside of me, making a way for Your love, comfort, and presence to be with me.

Thank You for not holding back and for giving everything You had so I could one day be with You forever! You are the perfect Father, the true Immortal Hero who saves us from ourselves. How I am blessed to be Yours!

Please, God, wrap Your arms around this world that needs You so much! I want to be one who demonstrates my love for You and Your love for others. Teach me how, God. I want to learn to love like You.

CHAPTER 11

Your Place in the Story

They will be called oaks of righteousness, a planting
of the LORD for the display of his splendor.

(Isa. 61:3b NIV)

As she lay across her bed, Kara's mind jumped from thought to thought. To Kara, the ceiling fan circling overhead was a perfect visual of her life: boring, monotonous, never ending.

Her eyes flitted to the framed pictures hanging on her walls … her cell phone with unanswered text messages … her laptop … clothes draped over the back of a chair … books from school reminding her of the work that must be completed before tomorrow morning.

Kara couldn't see outside the story of her life. Maybe at times you've felt this way as well.

She saw those books calling out again. Pressure to become, pressure to be, pressure to excel. Sometimes she wondered where she fit. It seemed like the world around her had centered on a bigger story than she saw in her life.

You know that feeling of disconnect when you walk into a room and don't know where you fit? When you feel the details of your life don't match up? You feel lost and alone in a crowd.

We all have this longing, way down deep inside, to connect. We want to feel settled. We want the assurance and comfort of belonging. We want to know we are somehow contributing, that our life counts and that others recognize that. The most amazing news for us is the fact that there is a story so much greater than our own, and we are invited to play a crucial part in it.

> "Next time a sunrise steals your breath or a meadow of flowers leaves you speechless, remain that way. Say nothing, and listen as heaven whispers, 'Do you like it? I did it just for you.'"—Max Lucado[1]

Ever wonder where your place is in the epic story? You have a carefully designed position, but often it is skewed by the Vampire's deceptions you have come to know and somehow trust. You have everything you need to resist his allure and entrapments; yet often you seek words of comfort on your own, pushing away from the One who loves you most.

✝ The most amazing news for us is the fact that there is a story so much greater than our own, and we are invited to play a crucial part in it. ✝

GETTING TO KNOW HIM

The greatest story of all involves a Hero who loves beyond all limits.

Unless you know someone—really know his heart—it's hard to trust his words and believe his love is true.

Remember how Edward first got to know Bella in *Twilight?* He was unable to read Bella's thoughts like he could everyone else's. In order to get to know her, he spent day after day talking with her, asking her questions.

He was interested in who she was, asking her about her likes, dislikes, relationships, and thoughts on different things. He wanted to know as much about her life as he could.

Edward's insatiable desire to know everything about Bella intrigued her. You would be crazy over this too, if someone cared that much about your every interest, if he wanted to know each of your thoughts so that he could better protect and honor you.

Just breathe ...

So just imagine if you could hear a story for the first time of a love beyond any you have ever heard. It describes how huge is the love and attentiveness of the true Immortal Hero. Listen to these words:

He will not let you stumble; the one who watches over you will not slumber. Indeed, he who watches over Israel [you] never slumbers or sleeps. The LORD himself watches over you! The LORD stands beside you as your protective shade. The sun will not harm you by day, nor the moon at night. The LORD keeps you from all harm and watches over your life. The LORD keeps watch over you as you come and go, both now and forever.

(Ps. 121:3–8 NLT)

What grabs my heart in these verses is that they point directly to Christ's perfect attentiveness and watchful care of us. Think about that. Look at how protective He is over your life.

And He wants you to know how much He understands you. He knows you and wants to hear your thoughts. He desires your full attention. He loves it when you share with Him about your hopes, your dreams, your heartbreaks, your fears. He is a personal and a magnificent God to whom no one can compare.

Equally important is the fact that He is available to you at all times. Through His Word, you have the opportunity to get to know Him. He is a multifaceted God. There is so much to know about Him. He is a God without limits, filled with mystery and intrigue.

> "A woman's heart should be so hidden in God that a man has to seek Him just to find her."—Max Lucado

He is also true and unchanging. His Word says so! "He is unchangeable.... Whatever he has desired, he does" (Job 23:13 NET). You can trust Him. His promises are true and everlasting.

KNOWING HIS VOICE

The greatest story of all involves a Hero who gives His heart.

His voice is so reassuring and peace giving to the deepest part of you that you'll want to hear His words. Many girls have asked me how they can know when God is talking to their hearts. Here is the best way I can describe it.

Think about your closest friends, the ones who know you best. You know how they think and feel, and you can almost hear their words in your head. You can pretty much guess what they're going to say next ... and it seems like they can almost read your mind.

Knowing friends that well comes from spending so much time talking with them. Also, it comes from walking through life experiences together.

It's the same way in your relationship with God. The more time you spend with Him, the more you'll understand His heart and what He thinks about you and your life.

Through reading His Word—His letters of love to you—you'll come to know how much you mean to Him.

Isn't it incredible that through His words and through conversations with Him in prayer, you can come to know His voice?

> ✝ The more time you spend with Him, the more you'll understand His heart and what He thinks about you and your life. ✝

> Call to me and I will answer you. I'll tell you marvelous and wondrous things that you could never figure out on your own.
>
> *(Jer. 33:3 MSG)*

One of the greatest things about having a close relationship with God is that you get to talk with Him about whatever is in your heart. He is always listening.

TRUST HIS LEAD

The greatest story of all involves a Hero who asks you to trust Him completely.

Trust is a gift that has to be given and received. We talked earlier in this chapter about how it is impossible to trust someone until you feel totally comfortable with them. You can't really trust until you are able to look into the eyes of a friend and share your heart without question.

Imagine trusting someone so much that your entire life rests on following His lead, on the decisions He makes for you. Seems like a pretty vulnerable thing to do, doesn't it? You may have a hard time imagining yourself ever trusting someone that completely.

Trusting Him doesn't mean that nothing bad will ever happen to you; rather, it means that when hard times come, you can know He will be with you every step of the way.

Learning how to trust Him takes …

- Listening to His words and depending on them.
- Talking to Him. *He wants to hear what you have to say!*
- Spending time with people who love Him too.

> Strive to know His heart. Once you come to know Him personally, to hear His voice, and seek His face, you'll trust Him and be willing to follow His lead. "Trust in the LORD with all your heart and lean not on your own understanding; in all your ways acknowledge him, and he will make your paths straight" (Prov. 3:5–6 NIV).

Choosing a life filled with God's presence, His beauty, and His peace means that you possess both hope and security. You belong; you are held securely in Christ. In Him, you can escape a lesser life filled with life-sucking disappointments and disillusions. In Him your life story takes on life-giving purpose and true adventure.

You and I are each part of a much bigger story—the story of God's epic love and His massive work in the universe throughout all time.

ENTER THE RESCUER

The greatest story of all involves a Hero who offers pure rescue.

Christ honored women. All throughout the Bible we see it. He chose them. He acknowledged them. He honored them. He showed them His love and

✦ Women are a part of God's story, their lives a constant proclamation of His amazing love. ✦

Look how much He cares for you! "Indeed, the very hairs of your head are all numbered. Don't be afraid; you are worth more than many sparrows" (Luke 12:7 NIV).

acceptance. He created them with purpose and wanted to see those purposes fulfilled. He came alongside them as they were hurting. As they spoke to Him, He listened. He defended their honor and believed in their future. He looked past their fears and failures and saw the people He had called them to be. He never once disrespected or dishonored. He loved. He comforted. He cherished.

Think about the women in the Bible and how their stories continue to teach and encourage. Women are a part of God's story, their lives a constant proclamation of His amazing love.

These historical stories reflect who He is and point us to the rescue of our hearts.

Just look at the way Jesus met them in their hurt and answered their hearts' deepest needs. Maybe their stories remind you of your own.

1. You may feel abandoned. Read John 4:1–26.

Jesus stopped to talk with a Samaritan woman at the well. In that time, Jews were not to talk to Samaritans. Instead of judging her, He showed her compassion in the middle of the sinful life she was leading. Jesus knew everything yet accepted her in the midst of her sin.

2. You may feel misunderstood. Read Matthew 26:6–13.

A woman poured her very expensive perfume on Jesus' head. He defended her as the men questioned what she was doing. He stood up for her heart.

3. You may feel unheard and burdened for someone else. Read Mark 7:24–30.

A woman's daughter was released of a demon. Jesus took time not only to heal her daughter but to hear her concern and teach her heart.

4. You may feel unappreciated. Read Luke 10:38–42.

Jesus took time to speak with Mary and Martha. He listened to Martha, who was frustrated and concerned. He gave her answers and took time to teach her. He cared enough to teach her what was on His heart, what she would need for the rest of her life. He also acknowledged her gift of serving.

5. You may feel forsaken. Read John 20:10–18.

Jesus chose Mary Magdalene to be the first one He spoke to after He rose from the dead. He met her in her tears and loss. He did not abandon her but left her with promise and hope. He met her out of all the people in the world.

And He meets you now. He longs to speak His strong words, to speak deeply into your life. He loves. He cares. He believes in who you have been created to be.

Just breathe …

So where do you see yourself in the story? Like the woman at the well, who felt alone and used? Maybe you feel like the woman who gave everything to God but still felt judged and misunderstood by others. Maybe you feel unheard and unappreciated. You can rest in this: Whatever you're experiencing, He knows your heart and offers unconditional rescue.

A HEART LIKE HIS

The greatest story of all involves a Hero who leads you on a path of righteousness for His name's sake.

Jessie's heart was drawn to her Immortal Hero. Life wasn't always easy, but she stayed true. She clung to His words as promises, and I watched her receive the blessings of obedience and trust. As she stayed close to Him year after year, she reflected His heart.

Eight years after I met her, I received this email. But it wasn't from Jessie.

To: Kimberly

From: Nathan

Subject: Thanks from the heart!

Dear Kimberly,

I am engaged to Jessie, who attended one of your conferences when she was in middle school. We are now both upperclassmen in college.

I have become more and more thankful for the impact that simple but powerful conference had on her. It was the seed that led to much of her initial understanding of God's unconditional love for her. She was introduced to ways of thinking about morals and purity at a young (but crucial) age.

Over the four years we have been together, I have come to especially cherish the beauty in her heart. Almost a decade later, we are both blessed by the impact that weekend had.

Obviously, not all of who Jessie is today is a result of that weekend, but the ripples are still widening. There have been times when she was the anchor in our relationship.

I have been especially moved lately to thank you for what you did early on in the heart of my future wife, and for how that has changed my own heart. In saying this, I know where all the glory goes, so thank you mostly for being His vessel; I'm sure I'm not alone in my gratitude.

In Him,
Nathan, Jessie's fiancé

What amazing words to read! Maybe one day your fiancé will write to tell me about how radically Jesus shaped you into the woman he fell in love with!

LIVE BEYOND YOURSELF

The greatest story of all involves a Hero who rescues you so that you can love like He loves.

Mother Teresa, a precious woman who lived in Calcutta, India, spent decades serving the poorest of the poor in the name of Jesus. Maybe you have heard about this remarkable woman who knew what it meant to live beyond herself. She was a Catholic nun who ministered for over forty years to the poor, the dying, the orphans, and the homeless. She radiated a true beauty that reached beyond her own life—and what a life she lived for others! Her story is amazing.

Picture an energetic woman less than five feet tall who spent her life caring for people everyone else in the world had forgotten. In her own words, she reached out in love "to those that have become a burden to society and are shunned by everyone." I told you she was amazing!

With a will of iron and a heart of love, she cared for thousands, many of who were close to death. She wanted these people to know that they were loved and wanted. She once said, "In this life we cannot do great things. We can only do small things with great love."

It took great courage for Mother Teresa to step out and love like Christ. Her place in the story was focused on tough love reaching the dying. What a reflection of His heart!

We can live life totally caught up in His love and attempt to keep it all to ourselves, or we can live life with a drive and focus beyond ourselves. Which will you choose?

During her lifetime, Mother Teresa touched thousands of people all over the world. Her efforts helped establish 610 Missionaries of Charity ministries in 123 countries around the world. She won a Nobel Peace Prize and was visited by royalty. Her life inspired others; *her life made a difference!*

God used her true beauty *inside* to make a difference in the lives of others. She shared this about her work: "We

When the Heart Speaks

"Being unwanted, unloved, uncared for, forgotten by everybody—I think that is a much greater hunger, a much greater poverty than the person who has nothing to eat."—Mother Teresa ourselves feel that what we are doing is just a drop in the ocean. But the ocean would be less because of that missing drop."

LIVE FORWARD

The greatest story of all involves a Hero who redeems you so that you can step forward in power and purpose.

The greatest mortal heroes through the ages have come and gone. Many are remembered for centuries because they made their marks on society and then died a brave death.

There is but one Immortal Hero of all time. He made an eternal impression. *That* was enough.

✜ "A planting of the LORD for the display of his splendor" (Isa. 61:3 NIV).... That's how God sees *you*. Your life, lived for Him, has all the potential to make a huge difference. ✜

If you catch a glimpse of this Hero, you will be changed. As you spend time with Him, your heart will be drawn, your focus redirected, and your life-giving future secured.

This is your future in Christ: "They will be called oaks of righteousness, a planting of the LORD for the display of his splendor" (Isa. 61:3 NIV). Think about that for a second: "A planting of the LORD for the display of his splendor." That's how God sees *you*. Your life, lived for Him, has all the potential to make a huge difference.

"Life is God's novel. Let Him write it."
—Isaac Bashevis Singer

Living forward means becoming more like Jesus and, in the process, forever escaping a captive, fearful life controlled by the Ultimate Vampire.

It's a mystery, actually—this life lived out in the freedom that the true Immortal Hero provides. You are given freedom to live a purposeful life established by who you are in Christ. It means that even when everything is crashing down all around you, you aren't rocked. Christ rescues you and sets you free for a purpose—and draws you into His epic story of love.

Just breathe ...

What an honor it has been to share about the amazing freedom found in Christ alone! I would love to hear from your heart on how you have come to know Him more through the pages of this book. If you'd like to share, send me a message through the *Escaping the Vampire* Facebook page! I'll keep praying for you, my friend. I just know He has great plans in mind—and He will continue to speak His words of love over your life. Trust the heart of your Hero. He loves you so much!

A Letter to Moms & Mentors

Dear Moms and Mentors,

I've been honored to walk through this book in conversation with your teen. Whether you're a mom, mentor, or youth leader—or if you have a teen girl you love in your life—thank you for sharing her with me. These conversations about eternal love and forbidden love, the joys and emotional pains in life and relationships, and our desire for rescue and escape are familiar to all of us.

I know you have fought through many of these struggles yourself—and still may have battles going on inside—so in many ways, you understand what your teen is facing. But isn't it interesting to see how some of the struggles impacting her today are so different from what you may have experienced? At times it may seem difficult to know how to relate.

Taking time to hear your teen's heart even when you may not always agree with her is such an essential part of building a lasting, trusting relationship. I'd like to encourage you to consider viewing life from her perspective. Pray that God would give you understanding and wisdom in your conversations. We can learn from each other. We can grow in relationship.

So grab your own copy of this book. (You'll need to because your daughter's copy is likely filled with confidential words from her heart!) Mark up your book with your own thoughts, prayers, ideas … you will see how these truths are vital for your life as well. I pray that it will be a wonderful connection point for you both.

Because it would be my privilege to continue coming alongside you and your teen, I've created some easily downloadable material that can be accessed on both my Web site (www.wttym.org) and David C. Cook's Web site (www.davidccook.com).

In this resource material, you'll find talking points, creative ideas for connecting with your teen, and key Scriptures that will take you through themes in the book. I've compiled thoughts that will inspire you toward deeper reflection, and you'll be challenged in your walk with God and your relationship with your teen. My hope is to advocate a heart connection between you and your teen, and for you both to continue growing closer to Christ, pursuing the Immortal Hero as He sweeps you up in His epic story of love.

It has been a blessing to share God's heart with you throughout this book. I would be honored to meet and pray with you and your teen at a conference event. I'll look forward to that day. In the meantime, be sure to keep checking the Web sites for more materials, blogs, and chats. Oh, and definitely look me up on Facebook by searching for "Escaping the Vampire." Hope to talk with you soon!

With many blessings and much love,
Kimberly

Notes

Chapter 1:

1. J. Gordon Melton, *The Vampire Book: The Encyclopedia of the Undead* (Canton, MI: Visible Ink, 1998), xvi.

2. "Vampire," *Wikipedia*, http://en.wikipedia.org/wiki/Vampire.

3. Melton, *The Vampire Book*, 108.

4. Melton, *The Vampire Book*, 109.

5. Margaret Carter, "What Is a Good Guy Vampire?" *Good Guys Wear Fangs* 1 (May 1992): vi–ix.

6. Ken Gelder, *Reading the Vampire*, in Jennie Yabroff, "A Bit Long in the Tooth," *Newsweek*, December, 2008.

7. "Vampire," *Wikipedia.*

8. James Wolcott, "The *Twilight* Zone," *Vanity Fair*, December 2008.

9. Jennie Yabroff, "A Bit Long in the Tooth."

10. Ken Gelder, *Reading the Vampire*, in Jennie Yabroff, "A Bit Long in the Tooth."

11. Beth Felker Jones, "Vampires and Young Female Desire," *The Gospel & Culture Project*, July 2, 2009, www.gospelandculture.org/2008/11/vampires-and-young-female-desire.

12. Diane Robina, in Christine Spines, "Bring on the Blood," *Entertainment Weekly*, July 3, 2009, 23–24.

13. "Kristen Stewart Draws from Real Love Life," *Shine On Media*, November 16, 2008, http://www.shineon-media.com/2008/11/16/kristen-stewart-draws-from-real-love-life.

Chapter 2:

1. Stephenie Meyer, "Frequently Asked Questions: *Twilight,*" The Official Web site of Stephenie Meyer, http://www.stepheniemeyer.com/twilight_faq.html.

Chapter 3:

1. "Healing Mothers and Daughters," *The Oprah Winfrey Show,* May 24, 2006, http://www.oprah.com/slideshow/oprahshow/oprahshow1_ss_20060424.

2. 2008 National STD Prevention Conference: Confronting Challenges, Applying Solutions, Department of Health and Human Services Centers for Disease Control and Prevention, http://www.cdc.gov/stdconference/2008/press/release-11march2008. htm (accessed August 8, 2009).

3. Frank Viola, *From Eternity to Here: Rediscovering The Ageless Purpose of God* (Colorado Springs, CO: David C. Cook, 2009), 87–88.

Chapter 4:

1. Floyd McClung, *The Father Heart of God* (Eugene, OR: Harvest House Publishers, 2004), 21

2. Claire Cloninger, *Dear Abba* (Birmingham, AL: New Hope Publishers, 2005), 31–32.

3. Philip Yancey, *What's So Amazing About Grace?* (Grand Rapids, MI: Zondervan, 2002), 71.

Chapter 5:

1. "Definition of Redemption," Access-Jesus.com, www.access-jesus.com/Hebrews/ Hebrews_9_12 (accessed August 19, 2009).

Chapter 6:

1. J. C. Ryle, "Calvary!" http://www.biblebb.com/files/ryle/calvary.htm.

Chapter 8:

1. J. J. Dewey, *Light and Dark Book of Quotes: Inspirational, Spiritual and Metaphysical Quotes from the Writings of J. J. Dewey*, www.freeread.com/archives/light-dark-quotes.php.

2. Ibid.

3. Ibid.

4. "Darkness," *Wikipedia*, http://en.wikipedia.org/wiki/Darkness.

5. "Light," *Dictionary.com*, http://dictionary.reference.com/browse/light.

Chapter 10:

1. "Kids Define 'Love'," *Great Dad.com*, http://www.greatdad.com/tertiary/295/690/kids-define-love.html.

2. Stephenie Meyer, *Twilight* (Boston: Little, Brown Young Readers, 2006), 274.

3. Viola, *From Eternity to Here*, 26.

4. C. S. Lewis, "The Weight of Glory," *Theology*, November 1941, http://www.doxaweb.com/assets/doxa.pdf.

5. Biblical Discernment Ministries, "Unconditional Love and Acceptance?" December 1997, http://www.rapidnet.com/~jbeard/bdm/Introduction/uncondit.htm, adapted from Martin and Deidre Bobgan, *Prophets of PsychoHeresy II* (EastGate Publishers, 1990), 91–96, and *PsychoHeresy Awareness Letter*, September–October 1997.

6. Viola, *From Eternity to Here*, 26.

Chapter 11:

1. Max Lucado, *Let the Journey Begin* (Nashville, TN: Thomas Nelson, 2009), 101.

in search of a princess™
a weekend celebration

Inspire teens to find their true identity in Christ.

This weekend celebration combines encouragement, energy, and personalized attention focusing on teen girls and their specific needs. Each girl discovers the unconditional love of her personal Father God and realizes His passionate pursuit of her heart. The girls are inspired and challenged to find their true worth and purpose in an intimate relationship with their heavenly Father!

Session themes are: The Dream of You; Claim the Beauty; Chocolate-Covered Secrets; Daddy, I Need You; Soul-Tie to the Father; Chosen to Dance; and The King's Wish

---

"Every morning when I woke up in the hotel I was eager to hear you speak. This weekend changed my life in so many ways that I couldn't list them all!"
— Teen attendee

Kimberly Powers is the executive director and co-founder of Walk The Talk Youth Ministries, Inc. (www.wttym.org) —a national nonprofit youth ministry which inspires teens to find their true identity in Christ, walking out their faith boldly in speech, in life, in love, in faith, and in purity.
(1 Timothy 4:12)